中华文化外译书系·民俗与区域文化

总主编 廖开洪

The Cowherd and the Weaver Fairy
A Study on the Folk Story and Double Seventh Day

七夕文化透视

赵逵夫 著　　赵晓燕 编译

厦门大学出版社 国家一级出版社
XIAMEN UNIVERSITY PRESS 全国百佳图书出版单位

图书在版编目（CIP）数据

七夕文化透视 / 赵逵夫著；赵晓燕编译. -- 厦门：
厦门大学出版社，2024.6
　　ISBN 978-7-5615-9163-5

　　Ⅰ．①七… Ⅱ．①赵… ②赵… Ⅲ．①节日-风俗习
惯-研究-中国 Ⅳ．①K892.1

中国国家版本馆CIP数据核字(2023)第207482号

责任编辑	高奕欢
美术编辑	张雨秋
技术编辑	许克华

出版发行　厦门大学出版社

社　　址	厦门市软件园二期望海路 39 号
邮政编码	361008
总　　机	0592-2181111　0592-2181406(传真)
营销中心	0592-2184458　0592-2181365
网　　址	http://www.xmupress.com
邮　　箱	xmup@xmupress.com
印　　刷	厦门市金凯龙包装科技有限公司

开本	720 mm×1 020 mm　1/16
印张	15
插页	1
字数	270 千字
版次	2024 年 6 月第 1 版
印次	2024 年 6 月第 1 次印刷
定价	60.00 元

本书如有印装质量问题请直接寄承印厂调换

厦门大学出版社
微信二维码

厦门大学出版社
微博二维码

Preface

In accordance with its mission of disseminating knowledge and promoting Chinese culture, Jinan University is dedicated to the great cause of promoting Chinese culture abroad. Our aim is to ensure that our voices are heard, our stories read, our culture understood, and our country respected. Grounded upon this background, the book series in English version "Classical Chinese Novels" and "Folk Customs and Regional Culture" are published to incorporate the appreciation of Chinese novels, the research on the relationship between Chinese novels and social institutions, local customs and culture, religion, and psychology, as well as the circulation of Chinese folk and regional culture, in an effort to spread Chinese culture. Involving universal cultural readings that highlight academic, intellectual, popular and accessible features with richly informative contents, the series are designated for foreign readers who are fond of Chinese culture.

The two book series are noticeably distinct from general academic works in that they not only aim to introduce comprehensive but diversified Chinese culture to the world, but also to introduce it in plain language with new ways of thinking and writing methods. In the series "Classical Chinese Novels", special attention is paid to the comprehensive study of philology, literature and art, especially the close reading of texts. Classical Chinese novels are explored

七夕文化透视 ▸▸▸
The Cowherd and the Weaver Fairy
A Study on the Folk Story and Double Seventh Day

from the perspective of culturology, while the relationship between classical Chinese novels and Chinese culture are observed in multiple dimensions. The series embraces the following main subjects: (1) close reading of the Chinese cultural works and their appreciation; (2) the classical novels and institutional culture; (3) the relationship between classical novels and religion; (4) the extraterritorial dissemination of classical novels; and (5) the comprehensive study of Chinese culture and psychology.

In the other series "Folk Customs and Regional Culture", colorful Chinese folk customs and regional culture are introduced and studied, in the hope of enhancing culture communication and mutual understanding. Taking *The Cowherd and the Weaver Fairy: A Study on the Folk Story and Double Seventh Day* as an example, the book starts with an analysis on the origin of the folk story "The Cowherd and the Weaver Fairy", one of the four best-known Chinese folk stories, and then proceeds with a folk custom study concerning the nationwide celebrations of Double Seventh Day (or the Qiqiao/Qixi Festival), which is supposed to honor the hero and the heroine of the story. Supported by the solid archaeological findings and convincing textual study on ancient literature, the book aims not only to provide readers with knowledge about the formation and development of the folk story as well as the regional evolution of the festival-related customs, but also promote the understanding and celebration of Double Seventh Day as an important traditional festival among modern Chinese. This is exactly an academic attempt to answer the contemporary call of "telling a good story about China".

Translation Studies, as a relatively young discipline in Jinan

University, was acknowledged as the "Outstanding Discipline" of Zhuhai City in 2015. Translation and Interpreting was entitled as the "Key Discipline" of Guangdong Province in 2018, and "the Construction Point of National First-Class Undergraduate Program" in 2021. Since the School of Translation Studies was founded in 2010, teachers have been granted twelve research projects sponsored by the National Social Science Fund of China. The School has also successfully trained students to compete in Hansuyin Youth Translation Awards, and has ranked first in the number of award winners among all the universities represented for three consecutive years. Achievements have been made in many respects, and more is to be expected in future.

We have invited teachers from our School as well as experts and professors from universities across China to participate in the translation and compilation of these two book series, among whom many have successfully translated more than twenty works related to Chinese culture. The translators of this book series are either experienced scholars in the prime of life or hard-working young scholars in their early academic years. In consultation with Jinan University Press, we have published "Translation of Chinese Cultural Works" (series) in a C-E bilingual edition in an effort to showcase the depth, classicalness and beauty of China's cultural history. Readers are sincerely welcomed to criticize, correct and make valuable comments and suggestions on these works.

Special thanks should be extended to all the colleagues of the School of Translation Studies who have made great contribution to the publication of the book series "Classical Chinese Novels" and "Folk Customs and Regional Culture", as well as the rapid development of the School of Translation Studies.

Kaihong Liao, Professor, Ph.D.,

Dean of the School of Translation Studies

Director of the Research Center for Translation

and Promotion of Chinese Culture, Jinan University

March 28, 2023

Contents

Introduction

The Qiqiao Festival[1], also called Double Seventh Day or the Qixi Festival, is an age-old traditional Chinese festival which is celebrated among not only people of Han nationality but also some Chinese ethnic groups, or even in other Asian countries such as Japan, Korea, Vietnam and parts of Southeast Asia. The origination of the festival can be traced back to as early as Warring-States period in history, first only celebrated in northwestern area, but later spread to the Central Plains and then nearly everywhere of the country.

---

[1] The Qiqiao Festival, which falls on the 7th of lunar July, was a very important festival in ancient China, especially for young girls. On the day, girls were granted a valuable chance to get together singing, dancing, and conducting their most important celebrations of Qiqiao rites in the evening under the moon. The celebrating rites and procedures vary from place to place, but the universal goal is to pray for blessings from Queen Qiao (the Weaver Fairy).

Figure 1　The Birthplace of Qiqiao Customs

by Lu Haiyan

The origination of the festival was closely related to geographical, seasonal, astronomic and atmospheric factors to which ancient Chinese was subject, but we should attribute its popularity to the influence of the folk story "The Cowherd and the Weaver Fairy" (牛郎织女的传说). When tracing back further, the early-stage fusion between Zhou and Qin tribal culture, especially the development history of the Qin tribe and the pre-Zhou history, shed new light on the festival's origin. During the evolution of the festival, rich, peculiar customs and rites have been developed.

The following is a probe into the origination and evolution of the folk story and the festival.

Chapter I
The Origin of the Folk Story "The Cowherd and the Weaver Fairy"

Section 1   Vega and Altair as well as Their Connection with Double Seventh Day (the Qiqiao Festival)

Astronomic factors, especially the location and movement of Vega ("the Weaver Fairy Star" as it's called in Chinese) and Altair ("the Cowherd Star" in Chinese) played a vital role in the origination and early spread of the festival.

Vega is a hyper-giant which is inferior in luminance only to Arcturus in the Northern Hemisphere. In ancient times, the moon and the bright stars served as the main light source, playing an important part in direction-giving during the night. Based on the movement model of the sun, the moon and the stars, people accumulated abundant astronomic knowledge and that about seasonal changes, thus building up their preliminary calendar system. Vega, one of the two brightest stars in the sky, and Altair, a superior-giant, were naturally among the first acknowledged and nominated stars to provide a coordinate for the observation and differentiation of other stars. In "The Record of Music and Calendar" from *The Book of the Han Dynasty* (*Hanshu*, 《汉书·律历志》), "Illustrations on Astronomical Vocabulary" from

七夕文化透视 ▸▸▸
The Cowherd and the Weaver Fairy
A Study on the Folk Story and Double Seventh Day

Erya (*Erya*,《尔雅·释天》)[①] and "The Record of Astronomy" from *The Book of the Han Dynasty* (《汉书·天文志》), there are very detailed explanations, definitions and illustrations on the evolution of the ancient astronomic system as well as the corresponding changes in the terms concerning Vega, Altair, Dipper and so on. From those early literature we can see that both Vega and Altair were of vital importance in the ancient astronomic coordination system, which provided people with basic guidelines in their agricultural production and social life. People's familiarity with the two stars in early history laid a foundation for the origination of the folk story.

Section 2   The Connection between the Folk Story "The Cowherd and the Weaver Fairy" & the Tribal Culture in Pre-Zhou and Early Qin Times

How did the Weaver Fairy Star (Vega) and the Cowherd Star (Altair) come by their personalized names in the first place? Up to now, the ancient and modern astronomers, researchers and annotators of *The Book of Songs* (*Shijing*,《诗经》) haven't given a satisfactory explanation to this question yet. After extensive literature research, I shared my opinion concerning this problem in two articles published in 1990, of which one is titled "On the Origination and the Motif of the Folk Story 'The Cowherd and the Weaver Fairy'" and the other "A Bridge between Folklore and Reality". In both the articles, I attributed the nomination of the second brightest star in the sky to the remotest ancestor Nüxiu (means Maid Xiu in Chinese) of the Qin tribe, which established the powerful Qin Dynasty in history. "The History of the

---

① *Erya* is regarded as the first dictionary in Chinese history which tries to explain and define the exact meaning of the ancient Chinese in graceful and official language.

Qin Dynasty" in *Records of the Grand Historian* (*Shiji*,《史记·秦本纪》) begins with the following sentences:

> Nüxiu (Maid Xiu, 女修), a female descendent of Emperor Zhuanxu (颛顼), gulped down an egg dropped by a swallow when she was weaving. She then gave birth to a baby boy who was later named Daye (大业).

Nüxiu was famous for weaving. As her story passed down through generations of her offsprings, she was sometimes lovingly called "the Weaving-maid Xiu". Her son, Daye, was the first male ancestor of the Qin people. The Milky Way was called "Han" (汉) in ancient times after the river by which the Qin people first inhabited. They named the Milky Way in the sky after the river in their hometown, and accordingly, named the brightest star to the north-west of the Milky Way after their remotest ancestor "the Weaver Fairy Xiu" as the Weaver Fairy Star.

As for the Cowherd Star (Altair), when I probed into this question in the 1980s, I believed that it was named to honor King Hai (王亥), the ancestor of the Shang tribe who established the Shang Dynasty in history. The repeated mention of King Hai "herding and taming cattle" in *The Classic of Mountains and Seas* (*Shanhai Jing*,《山海经》), *The Book of Pedigree* (*Shiben*,《世本》), *Chronological Records of History on Bamboo Slips* (*Zhushu Jinian*,《竹书纪年》), *A History by Lü Buwei* (*Lüshi Chunqiu*,《吕氏春秋》) and "Interrogations against the Heaven" ("Tianwen",《天问》) by Qu Yuan supports this opinion. But on further research, three questions caught my attention:

First, the early ancestors of the Shang tribe inhabited the Central Plains of ancient China which was far away from the early ancestors

七夕文化透视 ▶▶▶
The Cowherd and the Weaver Fairy
A Study on the Folk Story and Double Seventh Day

of the Qin tribe who lived in the southeastern area of now Gansu province, so it was very unlikely for their folk stories to merge into one in the early ages.

Second, "The Cowherd and the Weaver Fairy" tells a story set in a typical agricultural background where husbands planted and ploughed while their wives sewed and weaved. The accounts about "King Hai going to the North to trade with ethnic minorities for cattle" do not depict him as a farmer leashing a farm cattle, so they are not convincing enough to establish his identity as a farmer. This is because the ancestors of the Shang tribe mainly engaged in livestock breeding and husbandry at that time as their means of life, only settling down to an agricultural way after their intense conflict with the northern nomadic tribe Youdi (有狄). The oracle bone inscriptions recording Shang people's tradition of offering lavish sacrifices of livestock allow us a glimpse into their economic condition and cultural tradition.

Third, the legends concerning "cow-herding" in *The Book of Songs* are all related to the Zhou people.

In an article I published in 2004, "The Connection between the Han River and the Qiqiao Festival as well as the Relevant Festive Rites & Customs Practiced in Xihe and Lixian Counties of Gansu Province", I concluded my research with the following opinion: "The Cowherd was the ancestor of the Zhou people, Shujun (叔均), about whom there are three mentions in *The Classic of Mountains and Seas*. In "Inland Section" (《山海经·海内经》), it says: "Houji (后稷) started planting grains and his grandson Shujun was the first man to plough with cattle." This is a convincing proof for my opinion. Zhou people started planting on northwestern loess plateau very early and boasted of most developed agriculture among the big tribes in early Chinese history.

Another ancestor of the Zhou people, Buzhu (不窋), lived for a long time in the basin of the Malian River (马莲河) which flows through eastern Gansu province. According to *Kuodi Zhi* (《括地志》), "The ancient city Buzhu (不窋故城) was located about 1.5 kilometers to the south of Honghua county (弘化县) in Prefecture Qingzhou (庆州). That is where Buzhu once lived (at the end of the Xia Dynasty)." Honghua county of Prefecture Qingzhou, as it was called during the Tang Dynasty, is now Qingyang city in Gansu province. The early Zhou people named the bright star to the southeast of the Milky Way after their ancestor Shujun as "the Cowherd Star" to honor him for his contribution to agricultural production. According to professor Li Xueqin, a famous historian, the Zhou people first inhabited the area stretching from now Changwu county (长武县) in the western part of middle Shaanxi province to Qingyang city (庆阳市) in Gansu province. His idea is in concord with the existing archaeological discoveries made along the Jing and Wei rivers. This convinces us that the area extending from Huachi county to the north of Qingyang city southward to Qingyang, Heshui, Ningxian, jingchuan, Lingtai and Changwu of Shaanxi province was where ancestors of the Zhou tribe inhabited in early history. Nianzi Po, the place where over 230 graves from Pre-Zhou times were unearthed is located between Pingliang and Qingyang city in Gansu province, leaving a distance of less than 20 kilometers from its southeastern corner to Bin county of Shaanxi province.

What deserves our special attention is that among the unearthed articles in this area, bones of domestic animals abound, of which cow bones are the most numerous. This convinces us that cows were already an important domestic animal and the use of them in agriculture was very popular among the Zhou people. Among bone scriptures there was already a pictographic character specifically designed for "plough". Then it goes without saying that the Zhou people's application of cattle tillage originated before the Shang Dynasty. During the process of agricultural production, they started to keep domestic animals and applied them in tillage and transportation. This was a process of mutual-enhancement because when the domestic animals enabled them to improve work efficiency and produced good manure to their cropland, the leftovers from agricultural production served as good feed for the animals. Both agriculture and husbandry thus flourished.

As the Zhou and Qin people lived on bordering areas in early times, the contact and communication between them took place during the years between about 1054 BC and 896 BC, that is, under the reign of King Mu (穆王) and King Xiao (孝王) of the Western Zhou Dynasty. The ancestor of Qin people Zaofu (造父) bred battling horse for King Mu and was thus rewarded with a fiefdom in Zhao city (now the eastern Shanxi province), then his descendant Feizi (秦非子) did the same for King Xiao in the basin along the Qian River and the Wei River (in now Gansu and Shaanxi provinces), with a reward of fiefdom in Qin area (now part of Tianshui city, Gansu province). At the early years of the Eastern Zhou Dynasty, King Ping (平王) granted the land west to Qi (岐) (now northeastern part of Qishan county, Shaanxi province) to the Qin people. During the Spring and Autumn period, Qin tribe started expanding to the east, which guaranted more contact and communication between Qin and Zhou. Both peoples lived by the Han River which was named by the Qin people after where they had lived. When the story of the Cowherd was brought to the upper branch area to the Qin people, the two stories were told together and gradually united into one. The two bright stars which

were related to their ancestors respectively reminded the two peoples of the past which, when they gazed up into the night sky, ignited their imagination and spurred their artistic creation.

During the long years of cultural fusion between Qin and Zhou, the folk story "The Cowherd and the Weaver Fairy" finally came into being. The geographical background in the real world matches the plot in which the Cowherd and the Weaver Fairy are placed on the two sides of the Milky Way. This explains well why in Chinese, the word "Han" in the Han River has since been used to indicate the Milky Way. In most ancient literary works, in order to distinguish the Han River on the ground from the one in the sky, the word "celestial" was used in front of the word "Han" as "the Celestial Han River" when referring to the Milky Way. As we have discussed, it is a legacy from the early Qin culture. With the development and formation of agricultural society, Vega and Altair finally established their identity as "the Weaver Fairy Star" and "the Cowherd Star" in the connection with the folk story. The Cowherd and the Weaver Fairy, who represent the typical pattern of labor division between farming couples' under a self-sufficient frame of agricultural economy, embody at the same time numerous star-crossed lovers who were separated by force under the shackles of increasingly strict feudal ethics. The separation of the two stars by the Milky Way fueled people's wild imagination. When they put two and two together, the folk story emerged. The poem with "[t]he Cowherd star twinkles far far away, the Weaver Fairy dresses up in vain" as its opening sentence in *The 19 Classic Poems* (*Gushi Shijiu Shou*, 《古诗十九首》) of the Han Dynasty shows that the folk story had taken on its tragic ending by the Han Dynasty.

From "Dahuang Beijing" of *The Classic of Mountains and Seas* (《山海经·大荒北经》), there is a sentence which reads: "Shujun

七夕文化透视 ▶▶▶
The Cowherd and the Weaver Fairy
A Study on the Folk Story and Double Seventh Day

is the God of Cultivation." The two poems "Futian" (《甫田》) and "Datian" (《大田》) from "Classic of Poetry" in *The Book of Songs* (《诗经·小雅》), which were believed by the scholars including Zhu Xi (朱熹) to be the sacrificial poems in dedication to the God of Cultivation, provide a description on agricultural sacrificial rites through which people expressed their good will of having a year of favorable weather and a good harvest. Fang Yurun (方玉润) of the Qing Dynasty in his *Literary Research on the Book of Songs* (*Shijing Yuanshi*, 《诗经原始》) confirmed this conjecture. All those opinions support the idea that Shujun is the God of Cultivation in the image of Cowherd, the ancestor of Zhou people.

Those literary records together convince us that the folk story about the Cowherd and the Weaver Fairy as well as the relevant sacrificial rites originated very early in Chinese history. The earliest reference to the Cowherd and the Weaver Fairy can be read in *The Book of Songs*, especially in the poem "Dadong" (《诗经·小雅·大东》):

> The Milky Way glistens in the night
> like what's reflected from a mirror bright.
> The Weaver Fairy relocating seven times around the clock,
> produces no beautiful fabrics though fusses a lot,
>   —just like the Cowherd pulling no loads at all,
> as he is supposed to do so with a cow.

The metaphoric mention of the two stars in this poem proves that they were named as early as in the Western Zhou Dynasty. As the poem was written by a low-rank official of a small state Tan[1]

---

① The state Tan was located in now Shandong province.

satirizing the Zhou royal family which "gains without pains" through extorting excessive taxes and levies on the east vassal states, some researchers believe that by then, the folk story had not come into being yet. In my opinion, the two stars in the poem were regarded as two figures resembling ordinary couples on ground, of whom the wife engaged in sewing and weaving while the husband planting and tilling with cattle. The connection of the two figures with the Milky Way in the poem not only reveals the circulation of the folk story at that time but also tells us that the story were already known by the people in the eastern area during the Western Zhou Dynasty.

In "Ballads of the States" from *The Book of Songs* (《诗经·国风》), there are two other poems referring to the story (still in its primitive form) yet having escaped researcher's notice. Titled "A Woodcutter's Love" (《周南·汉广》) and "The Reed" (《秦风·蒹葭》) respectively, the former convinces us that the folk story had migrated from the northwestern China (to be exact, southern Gansu) along the Han River to southeastern China, and the latter backs up the belief that the story was circulating around the upper Han River basin among the early Qin people.[1] "The Reed" tells a story about a man who lingers along a river in pursuit of a beauty across the river in vain on a chilly morning in early autumn. The poem outlines the story of "The Cowherd and the Weaver Fairy" from the perspective of the Cowherd, depicting the Weaver Fairy as "a beauty across the river". In "The Woodcutter's Love", a man stands on the bank of the Han River looking at a beauty across the river, too. The poem begins with "The tallest southern tree

---

[1] In ancient times, the Eastern Han River and the Western Han River used to be the same river whose course was blocked during an earthquake at Lüeyang county in southwestern Shaanxi during the Western Han Dynasty, which led to the course change to the South and the division into two rivers later.

affords no shade for me. The maiden on the stream can but be found in dream."[1] The "tallest tree" symbolizes the high status of the maid who is beyond his reach, in accordance with the statements from "The Profiling of Officials in Heaven" from *Records of the Grand Historian* (《史记·天官书》): "The Weaver Fairy is the daughter of Queen of Heaven." The repeated lines in the second and the third stanza go like this: "Of the trees in the wood I will only cut the good." They manifest solidarity in the man's pursuit and his desire for the most outstanding girl. This poem is said to have been collected in the area surrounding the middle reach of the Han River which covers approximately the central Shaanxi province and the southeastern Hubei province.

The Qiqiao celebrations observed by the unmarried girls in some parts of Hanzhong city (actually the basin covering the middle reaches of the Han River) in Shaanxi province are held during the 3 days from the fifth to the seventh of lunar January, similar to that conducted in Longnan and Tianshui city of Gansu province (the southeastern area). In Yunxi county of Hubei province, there is a small area named "Celestial River" where the tradition of paying respect to Queen Qiao (巧娘娘)[2] and chanting Qiqiao songs on Double Seventh Day and the seventh of the lunar January is still observed.

We can thus obtain a more comprehensive picture when putting two and two together. No matter what, the spread of the folk story "The

---

[1]　According to the translation by Xu Yuanchong in *Book of Poetry*, Hunan Publishing House, 1993.

[2]　The word "Qiao" as in Queen Qiao, or in Qiqiao songs, is rich in connotative meaning which not only means "smart, skillful, deft in needlework and housework", but also delivers the young girls' wish for a Mr. Right, nice parents-in-law, and harmonious marital life or to be short, being happy in future. Thus it's hard to replace it with a single English word in translation.

Cowherd and the Weaver Fairy" from the Northwest along the Han River down to the Southeast should be regarded as a historical fact.

Section 3　Why Does the Qiqiao Festival Fall on the Seventh of Lunar July?

Why has the Qiqiao festival (Qixi, or Double Seventh Day) been celebrated on the 7th of lunar July? There are five reasons for that, of which two were proposed by a Japanese scholar Izuishi Masahiko (出石诚彦) more than 90 years ago, but failed to catch any attention since. In the following I will give a comprehensive explanation of those five reasons.

First, it is celebrated at the beginning of lunar July, that is, during the short farming break between the summer and autumn harvest. Many big tribes in early Chinese history transitioned from their primitive fishing and hunting mode of production into an agricultural economy after the foundation of the Xia and Shang Dynasties in succession. That's why China boasts a history of agricultural economy spanning over 4000 years.

"Twenty-four Solar Terms", the peculiar cultural creation of Chinese which helps in organizing production and daily life planning in an agricultural society, was designated as World Intangible Cultural Heritage in 2016. But "twenty-four solar terms" only mark the particular climatic changes for the Chinese, and are not celebrated as festivals. In fact, nearly all traditional Chinese festivals occur on days during farming breaks.

For example, lunar January in which the Spring Festival falls, and lunar December which is primarily dedicated to the preparations for the Spring Festival, are the two months which happen to liberate

七夕文化透视 ▶▶▶
The Cowherd and the Weaver Fairy
A Study on the Folk Story and Double Seventh Day

the diligent Chinese farmers from their labor for the longest time in the whole year. During this time, the farmers could visit their relatives and enjoy celebration performances till the 16th of lunar January. In some remote areas where villages were scattered, visits around with the scarce and backward transportation means were usually time-consuming, so the Festival visits there were sometimes prolonged till the beginning of lunar February. Other festivals such as the Dragon-boat Festival and the Mid-Autumn Festival also come during agricultural breaks. So it is with Double Seventh Day. "The Reed" describes a picture in which the Cowherd star meets the Weaver Fairy star at the beginning of lunar July when the "morning dew turned into white frost", exactly during a farming break.

Second, Izuishi Masahiko explained in his work *The Research on the Folk Story "The Cowherd and the Weaver Fairy"*: "Lunar July is the month when we have the best chance of observing stars in the clearest and purest night sky. The distance between the Cowherd star and the Weaver Fairy star is shortest in lunar July, suggesting a easy reunion of the couple." This provides a best explanation for the timing of the Festival.

Third, Izuishi Masahiko explained in the same work: "Supported by the age-old idea of Five Elements, the Chinese tended to arrange various activities and celebrations on the 1st of lunar January, the 3rd of lunar March, the 5th of lunar May and the 9th of lunar September. The celebration of Double Seventh Day when the two stars are closest to each other aligns with this idea, thus is a perfect choice." He additionally cited several other stories about the meeting couples on the day to support his idea.

Fourth, the number 7 started to take on the connotation of "return/ reunion" as early as in *The Book of Changes* (Zhouyi,《周易》), which may be the result of the particular arrangement of the Double Divination in Bagua (Eight Trigrams, 八卦) in which a new trigram starts following the sixth divinatory symbols of the previous trigram. A new start following the sixth (that is, the seventh) in the sequence means "return to the very beginning". Hence, the connection between the number 7 and "return/reunion" originated from a very early time. From then on, the mention of the number 7 in literature, whether referring to "every other 7 days" or "the 7th of a month", is always connected with the concept of return or reunion.

Among the bamboo relics unearthed in Number 11 Qin tomb in Shuihu Di, Yunmeng county of Hubei province which are believed to belong to a period ranging from the end of the Warring States to the 30th reigning year of Emperor Qin Shihuang (秦始皇), there are two pieces from *The Almanac*[①] (*Rishu*, or *The Book of Days*,《日书》), which record the story "The Cowherd and the Weaver Fairy". Number 155 bamboo slip reads:

> Wushen and Jiyou[②] are the days when the Cowherd married the Weaver Fairy. Their marriage didn't work out, as the Weaver Fairy walked out on the Cowherd three years later.

This is the earliest most clearly phrased version of the story. As it was mentioned that the Weaver Fairy "walked out on the Cowherd", the arrangement of the couple's reunion on the 7th of lunar July is quite understandable then.

① A book which tells people whether it's auspicious or inauspicious, fit or unfit, to do something on certain days. It's like a book of divination.
② In ancient China, 12 Earthly Branches (Dizhi, 地支) were used in combination with 10 Heavenly Stems (Tiangan, 天干) to designate years, months, days and hours, which, marked with certain combinations, run in cycles of sixty. Wushen and Jiyou are two days designated in this way.

七夕文化透视 ▸▸▸
The Cowherd and the Weaver Fairy
A Study on the Folk Story and Double Seventh Day

Fifth, in the essay "On Working Principles of Five Elements in the Human Body" of the medical classic *Su Wen*[①] (*Huangdi Neijing*, 《黄帝内经·素问·五常政大论》), in its annotations by the scholars of later ages and in other literary records, there are repeated mentions of the number 7's connection with the West. Astronomic changes of the two stars show that according to the earliest account of the folk story, the reunion of the couple on which the Cowherd crossed the Milky Way (moving westward) to meet the Weaver Fairy takes place on the west bank of the Milky Way. That's probably another reason for setting the Festival on the 7th of lunar July.

Section 4　Reunion over the Magpie Bridge and the Evolution of the Qiqiao Festival

The festive customs on the Qiqiao Festival are closely related to the reunion of the couple over the magpie bridge. According to "A Woodcutter's Love" and "The Reed" from *The Book of Songs* as well as *The Almanac* from the bamboo relics of the Qin Dynasty, the couple were separated from each other for unknown reasons without mentioning their reunion. But judging from the existing literary records, the plot of reunion had already come into being before the Qin Dynasty.

According to the account in important geographical work *Sanfu Huangtu* (《三辅黄图》) written around the end of the Eastern Han Dynasty and the beginning of Wei times, Emperor Qin Shihuang ordered his Xianyang Palace (咸阳宫) to be built after the Purple Palace of the Jade Emperor, the fairy ruler of Heaven, in the sky. As there was no real Purple Palace for the builders to copy, they

---

①　*Su Wen* is part of *The Yellow Emperor's Classic of Internal Medicine*.

diverted the Wei River into Xianyang city and built a bridge over it to symbolize the meeting place of the Cowherd and the Weaver Fairy, that is, the magpie bridge, in order to enhance the analogy between the two emperors. The record convinces us that the folk story was already very popular among the Qin people (possibly known to other countries or areas as well) by then. The story had taken on the basic plotline in which the two united as a couple, but were later separated from each other by the Milky Way.

From the words "the Weaver Fairy went across the Milky Way to meet the Cowherd", we can see that at that time, the Weaver Fairy played a dominant role between the couple, which coincided with her identity as the granddaughter of Emperor Zhuanxu. After the Qin and Han Dynasties, during the gradual transformation of the story, Emperor Zhuanxu was either replaced by the Jade Emperor in Heaven, or the Weaver Fairy was believed to be the granddaughter of Queen Mother of the West. The word "West" in the latter's title coincides again with the early history of Qin people in northwestern China, to be exact, Gansu province.[1]

Emperor Qin Shihuang's attempt to present himself as the Highest and only ruler of the country was quite obvious, but at the same time, the memory of the Qin people about their shared past is reflected, too. From this we can deduce that the folk story must have been familiar to the Qin people, though whether the bridge over the Wei river was really intended as a symbol of magpie bridge remains a mystery, as no existing historical record suggests that.

In my opinion, it is quite probable that the imagination of a

---

[1]   There is a temple dedicated to Queen Mother of the West on the Mountain Hui of Jingchuan county, Gansu province. It is quite near Qingyang, the early habitat of the Qin people.

七夕文化透视 ▸▸▸
The Cowherd and the Weaver Fairy
A Study on the Folk Story and Double Seventh Day

"magpie bridge" existed before the Qin Dynasty. For Chinese of Ancient Times, it would be unlikely for the Weaver Fairy, a noble lady and the granddaughter of the Jade Emperor, to cross the Milky Way to meet the Cowherd in his shabby conditions. Later, in the Western Han Dynasty, when Confucianism prevailed the society and the idea of "Male's superiority over female" become entrenched, women then were supposed to go to their husbands' place for meetings, not vice versa. It was in this background that the Weaver Fairy started to cross the Milky Way to meet the Cowherd, about which abundant poems were written during Wei and Jin dynasties. Another question arises: "How could a person without magical power cross the Milky Way?" Ancient Chinese provided a ready answer out of their own life experience and observations on daily life: birds are equal to this task. Among the birds capable of high altitude flight, magpies exhibited amazing building skills and their habit of setting a piece of wood across in nest-building is especially impressive! Although the earliest observation of this behavior was recorded in *Youyang Zazu* (《酉阳杂俎》) by Duan Chengshi of the Tang Dynasty, most probably, people had come to realize this fact at an earlier time.

Another example of primitive imagination about flocking birds carrying people up into the sky can be found in "The Departing Sorrows" ("Lisao",《离骚》) by Qu Yuan of the Warring States period, where the author ascended into the sky on a flock of phoenixes guided by a white dragon. In *The Classic of Mountains and Seas*, there is a sentence: "There are flocks of colorful birds (phoenixes) on top of Jiuyi Mountain, which cast in motion extended shadows on the ground below." The frequent cultural contact between the Qin and Chu areas during the Spring and Autumn period as well as the Warring States period helped spread the imagination of birds carrying

people up into the sky. Thus, the plot involving the couple's reunion over a magpie bridge emerged.

The earliest account about a magpie bridge can be found in a quotation from *Huainan Zi* (《淮南子》) compiled in the Western Han Dynasty in *Encyclopedic Compilation of Best Bits from Classics and Historical Records* by Bai Juyi (*Baishi Jingshi Shilei*,《白氏经史事类》): "Magpies flocked above the Milky Way to make a bridge for the Weaver Fairy." This indicates that the plot of meeting on a magpie bridge existed as early as in the Western Han Dynasty. A quotation from *A General Introduction to Folk Customs* (*Fengsu Tongyi*,《风俗通义》) by Ying Shao of the Eastern Han Dynasty in *A Record of Folk Customs in Four Seasons* (*Suihua Jili*,《岁华纪丽》) by Han E of the Tang Dynasty reads like this: "The Weaver Fairy crosses the Milky Way on the evening of Double Seventh Day on a bridge held up by flocking magpies." *A General Introduction to Folk Customs* is a book dedicated to records of various social customs and traditions, thus is a reliable proof justifying the mention of magpie bridge in *Huainan Zi*.

A relevant question arises regarding when people started observing Qiqiao customs in history.

Based on the existing records, the Qiqiao custom of putting thin silk thread through tiny needle eyes under the moonlight to pray for blessings was already observed by imperial concubines and palace maids at the beginning of the Western Han Dynasty. Since the rule of the Western Han Dynasty was newly established, it was unlikely a custom exclusively observed by ladies in royal living quarters. Instead, it was likely a folk custom brought into the royal quarters by imperial concubines from outside. Ge Hong, in the first volume of his work *A Miscellaneous Work from Chang'an* (*Xijing Zaji*,

七夕文化透视 ▶▶▶
The Cowherd and the Weaver Fairy
A Study on the Folk Story and Double Seventh Day

《西京杂记》), a historical work on social customs of the Western Han Dynasty, wrote: "The royal ladies of the Han court practiced the custom of threading 7 needle eyes on Kaijin Pavilion. Everyone took part in the game." This is the earliest record concerning Qiqiao custom, leaving the origin earlier than that a mystery. The two poems "A Woodcutter's Love" and "The Reed" obviously focus on the theme of love between a farmer of a lower social rank and a lady from a high social status. When these storys and the related customs were introduced into the royal quarters where the concept of free love was a taboo, only the festive customs observed in outside society were kept for entertainment. As the emperor's women had endless leisure time to kill, they enjoyed needle-threading competition, Qiqiao songs singing and dancing on the evening of lunar July 7th. Later the imperial concubines developed a new custom that catered to their own wishes and showed their common concern: praying for male offspring at the Son-Giving Pond (百子池). This was a new turn in the development of the festive customs.

It has always been true that the ideology of the ruling class prevails in the whole society. As Confucianism emerged as an increasingly important ideological power after the Western Han Dynasty, the concept of men's superiority over women was commonly accepted. After the Wei and Jin times, the Dominant Family System (门阀制度) as an overwhelming administrative power ruled out the possibility of the union between a farmer and the granddaughter of the Jade Emperor at all. This turned the folk customs concerning Double Seventh Day into a pure festive activity in which young girls got together and prayed to the Queen Qiao for blessing (especially good luck in marriage) and superior skills in needlework (one of the highly valued virtues for girls in feudal China). Another interesting finding, though, is supported by the existing Qiqiao songs collected in *Xihe Qiqiao Songs* (《西和乞巧歌》) by my late father, Mr. Zhao Zixian, revealing that girls not only prayed for Mr. Right, or good needlework skills in Qiqiao activities through singing and dancing, but also expressed their concerns about social problems as well as their hatred toward social evils.

In the third volume of *A Miscellaneous Work from Chang'an*, the author wrote:

On the 1st of lunar July[1], the royal ladies would gather in the temple of Queen Qiao (the Weaver Fairy) to offer sacrifices. They would play flute Zhu[2], singing the song "Shangling" (《上灵》) before joining hands together and stamping their feet rhythmically to the song "Come the Fiery Phoenix". On the 7th of lunar July, they would play grandiose tunes by the Son-Giving Pond. When the music subsided, they would tie colorful silk threads on each other's wrist for good luck.

---

[1] In the existing edition, it is "October" instead of "July", but researchers have reached a consensus that it might have been caused by a transcription mistake, as "July" fits the logic better here.

[2] An ancient percussion instruments.

七夕文化透视 ▶▶▶
The Cowherd and the Weaver Fairy
A Study on the Folk Story and Double Seventh Day

Figure 2 Get–together Praying

by Zhao Jinhui

Figure 3 Welcoming Rite

by Zhao Jinhui

This is a description of the festive activities conducted in the royal court at the beginning of the Western Han Dynasty when the celebration started on the 1st of lunar July. As mentioned above, the customs of offering sacrifice as well as singing and dancing in honor of Queen Qiao were all observed in the following ages as common social practice, though varied in details from place to place. The song "Come the Fiery Phoenix" has been lost, but based on its title, it appears to be similar to "Come the Queen Qiao", the opening song sung by girl celebrants in Xihe and Lixian counties of Gansu province where the ancestors of the Qin people inhabited in ancient times. No surprise, Phoenix was the totem worshiped by the Qin people. This explains well why the Weaver Fairy's descending to the mortal world was depicted to take place on the back of a phoenix. Royal ladies in the Western Han court celebrated Double Seventh Day from the 1st to the 7th of lunar July, and this tradition continues today with the girl celebrants who are descendants of the Qin people in the areas of their ancestral habitat, such as Xihe and Lixian counties. The girl celebrants in Xihe and Lixian counties still keep the custom of taking turns to guard the praying site and the model of Queen Qiao during the festival. The girls from different celebration venues exchange visits as a tradition under the name of "Xing Qing" (行情), which means "escorting our goodwills to your place". Wherever they go, the girls sing and dance together, showcasing their artistic talents and challenging each other in composing Qiqiao song.

Figure 4 Sacrifice Offering

by Zhao Jinhui

Figure 5 Entertaining and Worshiping

by Zhao Jinhui

From what have been discussed above, we can see that folk customs related to Double Seventh Day and its celebrations have been in existence since Pre-Qin times, but the practice of praying for blessings started to take center stage at the beginning of the Western Han Dynasty. The festive customs now observed in Xihe and Lixian counties still follow the ancient procedures passed down from the Han Dynasty in general, in which girls dedicate themselves to a celebration lasting for 7 days and 8 nights singing, dancing, stomping their feet rhythmically and offering sacrifices to Queen Qiao to pay their respects.

Figure 6 Worshiping Queen Qiao

by Zhao Jinhui

七夕文化透视 ▶▶▶
The Cowherd and the Weaver Fairy
A Study on the Folk Story and Double Seventh Day

Figure 7 Fortune–telling with Bean Sprouts

by Zhao Jinhui

Figure 8 Seeing Off

by Zhao Jinhui

Section 5　The Connection between Double Seventh Day and the Culture of the Qin Tribe

From the end of the 1980s to the beginning of the 1990s, a great number of archaeological findings of Pre-Qin times were made at the hill Dabu Zi of Lixian county, Gansu province. The amazing abundance of the burial objects covering the hill convinced the researchers that it must have been the graveyards of royal families which once inhabited this area. The later archaeological study suggested that the objects were most probably from the Qin Dynasty. According to "The History of the Qin Dynasty" from *Records of the Great Historian (Shiji,*《史记·秦本纪》), Feizi (秦非子), the creator of the Qin state, was dispatched to Qin area by King Xiao of the Zhou Dynasty (周孝王). In the book, it says: "Feizi was allowed to resume the sacrifice to the ancestral temple of the Ying family, so he was called Qinying." It also records that the descendant of Qinzhong (秦仲) was conferred the title "the Minister of Western Area" (西垂大夫) by King Xuan of the Zhou Dynasty (周宣王). In *The Annotation* (《正义》), a quotation from *Kuodi Zhi*, a geographical work of the Tang Dynasty goes like this: "Longxi county (means "west to Long Mountain" and is between now Gansu and Shaanxi provinces) is located 90 *li* (45 kilometers) southwest to Shanggui county of prefecture Qin." These historical records convinced me that the graves unearthed in Dabu Zi hill of Lixian county must have belonged to the ancestral kings and pioneers of the Qin state. Relating this to the statement at the opening sentence of *Records of the Great Historian: History of Qin*, "Nüxiu, the ancestor of Qin people was good at weaving", we can conclude that the Weaver Fairy in the folk story actually refers to Nüxiu. I illustrated in two essays my belief that the Cowherd is the idolized ancestor of the Zhou people and the Weaver Fairy is that of the Qin people. The folk story is the result of a culture mix between the two tribes residing in neighbouring area around Tianshui and Longnan cities in Gansu province. So it is most probable that the folk story "The Cowherd and the Weaver Fairy" was first told among people dewelling in the aforementioned area including Tianshui, Longnan and Longdong (east to Long Mountain) areas. The relevant festive customs were most probably the relics of the sacrificial rites conducted by the Qin people when paying respects to their ancestors. Besides, the existing records featuring the folk story with an identifiable plot are all related to the living area of the Qin people.

The Qin culture of early times was closely related to the folk story "The Cowherd and the Weaver Fairy" as well as Double Seventh Day. They are so indispensable to each other that we can not study them separately. A comprehensive perspective is helpful in establishing a convincing connection between the archaeological findings of this area and the ceremonious festive celebrations of 7 days and 8 nights which have been conducted up to now in the corresponding area. More accounts in *Records of Grand Historian* and other historical works present details in accord with the information concerning ancestral temples and cultural relics of ancient Qin people in early history. A story about the couple Xiaoshi, a master flute-player and Nongyü, the daughter of King Mu of State Qin (秦穆公), which was recorded in *The Biographies of Fairies* (*Liexian Zhuan*, 《列仙传》), features a Lady Phoenix in "Qin people built a temple dedicated to Lady Phoenix in Yong county", which somewhat coincides with the recordings in *Annotations to The Records of Grand Historian* (*Shiji Jieji*, 《史记集解》) about a temple

of Lady Bao: "There is a Temple of Lady Bao in Chencang county where the lady has a meeting yearly, or every other year, with immortal Ye (叶君神). Whenever the latter comes, thunders boom and phoenix serves as his mount." In my opinion, these are actually the variations of the story "The Cowherd and the Weaver Fairy".

The name of the Mountain "Qi", which is near Changdao and Yanguan in Lixian county, means "praying for oracles through the offering of sacrifice". The right part of Chinese character "Qi" means "live in compact communities". According to historical records, the Mountain Qi standing at the upper reaches of the Han River happened to be where the Qin pioneers worshiped their ancestors. That's why the Qin people took the area along the Yang River, a branch of the Han River, as the place of their origin.

The connection between the folk story and the Han River, as well as the ancestral temples worshiped by Qin people perfectly explains the origination of Double Seventh Day and the relevant festive customs observed in this area. Of course, the eastward migration of Qin people left its traces along the way in the above-mentioned cities like Gui, Chencang, Pingyang, Yong and Xianyang cities in the form of festive customs which were gradually brought to Chang'an and its surrounding areas no later than the Qin and Han Dynasties and thus recorded as Qiqiao customs practiced in the Han court. It goes without saying that each compact community celebrating Double Seventh Day along the way from Xichui (means "the Western Area") to Chang'an would have contributed to the spread of the customs.

The folk customs about Double Seventh Day which originated in the Northwest were brought to the Central Plains with the move of the capital from Chang'an eastward to Luoyang no later than the Eastern Han Dynasty, and further spread to the East and the South at

七夕文化透视 ▸▸▸
The Cowherd and the Weaver Fairy
A Study on the Folk Story and Double Seventh Day

the end of the Eastern Han Dynasty and the beginning of the Wei and Jin times. After the chaos caused by consecutive wars and southward move of the capital to Nanjing during the Western and Eastern Jin Dynasties which was followed by the turmoil continued at the end of the Jin Dynasty and during the Southern and Northern Dynasties, people continued large-scale migration during the Sui Dynasty and after the collapse of the Tang Dynasty. The nationwide continuous cultural, economic and population exchange brought Double Seventh Day and its festive customs to every corner of the country, though varied in details according to specific natural and social conditions, or in some cases different social status. As several large-scale migrations to the south during major social turmoils after the Wei and Jin Dynasties were mostly populated by influential, privileged families of scholars and officials (the later so-called "Hakkas", 客家人), the festive celebrations of the South are tinted strongly with upper-class flavor in contrast with that practiced in the North. The differences in climate, geographical conditions, local products and folk customs lent more regional color to the festival customs.

During the Ming and Qing Dynasties, Double Seventh Day was celebrated among most of the population, even among some ethnic minority groups. By then, the festival was already ranked along with the Qingming Festival (the Tomb-Sweeping Festival), the Dragon Boat Festival, the Mid-Autumn Festival and the Double Ninth Festival as one of the major traditional festivals observed ceremoniously among the Chinese.

A comprehensive study on nationwide festive customs concerning Double Seventh Day reveals that from ancient times till today, it has always been a festival mainly observed by unmarried girls, so was regarded as a festival dedicated to girls in many areas.

Virtues and ideologies like frugality, sincerity, industriousness in acquiring working skills are highlighted in the celebrations. My late father Zhao Zixian, under the influence of New Movement of Folk Songs, organized his students in collecting Qiqiao songs in circulation in and around Xihe county (covering the area Mountain Qi and Yanguan of Lixian county at that time) in the 1930s. In the celebration lasting for 7 days and 8 nights, girls not only expressed their innermost desires and prayed for blessing from Queen Qiao on personal well-being and superior working skills, but also showed their concerns on social reality[①]. Even today, the festive customs are still helpful in encouraging girls to pursue personal happiness, in committing girls to family and social lives, or at a more macro level, in concocting a more harmonious society. What's most splendid about the festival is that all those which are not fulfilled through poker-faced lecturing or admonishment are achieved through the girls' active participation in a relaxing, happy, enjoyable atmosphere perpetuated by the age-old Chinese cultural spirit and long-established cultural tradition which had originated from remote times and been handed all the way down to the modern day. In this sense we can say that Qiqiao Festival has far-reaching social influence and is thus rich in social implications.

The colorful festive customs on Double Seventh Day observed in different regions of the country have been recorded in various classics and literary works. As the transmission and transformation of the festival as well as the differentiation in forms and contents of celebrations will be reserved for later discussion, I will save my words here.

---

①   For reference, please consult the book *Xihe Qiqiao Songs* (《西河乞巧歌》) by my late father Zhao Zixian.

七夕文化透视 ▸▸▸
The Cowherd and the Weaver Fairy
A Study on the Folk Story and Double Seventh Day

Section 6   The Han River, the Celestial Han River and Tianshui City[①]: On the Formation of the Weaver Fairy Story

Now that we have had enough discussion above on questions concerning the hero and the heroine of the folk story, it's better now to proceed the study from two perspectives: one macro and the other micro, with every effort made in finding clues in ancient literature while paying due attention to the circulation of the folk story, as well as the evolution of relevant customs. The latest archaeological findings and results of academic study should also be kept in mind. On the basis of a complete understanding of economic and cultural conditions of different regions in ancient times, we should sort out the earliest, most original records involving the main plot of the story while excluding all later-day variations and far-fetched additions.

On several drama adaptations in the early 1950s, my teacher Yang Sizhong (杨思仲 , also write under a pseudonym Chen Yong [陈涌]) published an essay titled "On the True Motif of 'The Cowherd and the Weaver Fairy' Story". He pointed out in the essay that "the Cowherd" and "the Weaver Fairy" represent the farming couples in our traditional agricultural society who have been planting and weaving for thousands of years. The occurrence of the story shouldn't be taken as accidental in history of folk literature, nor should we regard the characters and plots the reflections of particular cases alone. So when trying to determine where and when it originated, we should on the one hand rely on the earliest records, and on the other hand identify the very origin of the two images by their distinguishing features among ancient tribes which provides a convincing evidence for the existence of these two figures within a specific natural environment and economic structure.

① The name Tianshui means in Chinese "the City of Celestial River".

Two facts are now clear:

First, from the poem "Dadong", we can see "the Cowherd" and "the Weaver Fairy" had been used to name two stars on the two sides of the Milky Way, though no traces of a story attached to them have been found yet.

Second, judging from the ancient custom of naming stars after luminous tribal members such as Xuanyuan (轩辕), Zhu (柱, the son of Lieshan Shi [烈山氏], the earliest god of grains), Zaofu (造父), Fuyue (傅说), Wangliang (王良), Xizhong (奚仲), etc., who were either outstanding leaders, or great contributors to the tribe, it was most probably the case with Nüxiu, the earliest ancestor of Qin people, too. Besides, Daye, the son of Nüxiu, who was also the earliest male ancestor of Qin people, played a key role in the tribe's social transformation from matrilineality to patrilineality. Nüxiu, a female descendent of Emperor Zhuanxu, matched the identity of the Weaver Fairy who was believed to be the daughter of the Jade Emperor, or the granddaughter of Queen Mother of the West. Furthermore, the fact that she is distinguished in historical records as a weaver is of special importance to connecting her to the later-day Weaver Fairy.

We have discussed the historical sources regarding the identity of Nüxiu as the prototype of the Weaver Fairy in Section 2 of the chapter and the archaeological discoveries made around the upper branch of the Han River which is in the Southeast of Tianshui city (traditionally named as the prefecture Qin [秦州]). The identification of the numerous tombs, abundant serial bells, bronze tripods, and burial pottery models of chariots and horses typical of the Qin Dynasty have been confirmed one by one since 1987 as belonging to the ancestors and kings of Qin tribe in early times. From this we can see that the folk story is from the very beginning connected with the Han

River which shares the same word "Han" as in the Celestial River in ancient Chinese. Apart from these, another convincing proof is the ceremonious modernday celebrations held in Xihe and Lixian, the early habitats of the Qin tribe in history.

Xihe and Lixian counties located to the southeast of Tianshui city have a long tradition of celebrating Double Seventh Day in such a ceremonious way that it is rarely matched anywhere else. Approaching the end of lunar June, girls from both urban and rural areas organize themselves into groups of 20 to 30, based on the scale of neighborhood or village they live. They choose a spacious household to set up an altar for Queen Qiao, in which they would seat the paper model of Queen Qiao they "have escorted" from the local paper goods shop. With a grand "welcome ritual" on the 1st of lunar July, the Festival, which will last 7 days and 8 nights, opens solemnly. From the 1st to the 7th of lunar July, a series of rituals are conducted in a orderly manner, including Sacrifice Offering, Qiqiao Song Chanting and Visit-Exchanging (during which girls from different groups, villages and neighbourhoods will exchange visits, competing in Qiqiao-song singing to learn from each other for improvement). On the concluding day, i.e. the 7th of lunar July, after a grand dinner party and a rite of praying to Queen Qiao for happiness and superior domestic skills through bean sprouts pattern decoding, they go to the Yang River (a branch of the Han River) or the Han River itself, or whichever river they live nearby. Untieing the colorful silk-thread bracelets that they have been wearing since the Double Fifth Festival from their wrists, they connect them all together to make a rope which is long enough to span the river, symbolizing the bridge on which the couple meets. Finally, they conclude the 7-day-long Festival with a farewell ritual by burning the paper model of Queen Qiao by the riverside.

手绊搭桥

Figure 9　Building a Bridge with Silkthread Bracelets for Queen Qiao at Seeing–off Rite
by Lu Haiyan

七夕文化透视 ▸▸▸
The Cowherd and the Weaver Fairy
A Study on the Folk Story and Double Seventh Day

Nowhere else is the Festival celebrated in such a ceremonious and passionate way. New Qiqiao songs are composed every year, adding to the old ones in Xihe and Lixian counties, which show regional differences in both theme and style, thus contributing a lot to the development of local folk songs. Apart from the Qiqiao songs circulated in Xihe county which are quoted in Chapter 2, the following are several from Lixian county and the area surrounding Tianshui city. The first three were collected from Yongxing village in the south of Lixian county. The following is the first section of the one titled "Combing Song" (《梳头歌》):

> One bowl, two bowls,
> pomade I use for hairdo of Queen Qiao's.
> A dragon in the front and a city in the back,
> it goes quite well with the lips painted red.
> ...
> In silk red shoes and through the Southern Heaven Gate,
> Queen Qiao descends to join us in big feast.
> Come down to us! Come down to us!
> Dear Queen Qiao I love you so much!

"Embroidering Song" (《扎花歌》):

> Queen Qiao's face, a red red rose,
> Queen Qiao's eyes, twinkling twinkling pearls.
> Under the brightest star in the night sky,
> the sisters of the Wangs' in embroidery they outshine.

The eldest embroiders a big big rose,

The second a peony with emerald leaves.

Only the third sister a green hand at this,

but she can do weaving with great ease.

With cotton thread weighing one and half *jin*①,

she wants to trade for silk thread pins.

...

Rainbow colors are what she wants,

they present birds so lively for eagle to hunt,

Icy blue thread is another must to buy,

which makes animal embroidering such a easy try.

Ten lotuses are embroidered one by one,

among which nine but one flowering when done.

Then I took the bud to the hill,

where it blossoms in the morning chill.

Come down to us, come down to us!

Teach me embroidering thus and thus.

Come down to us, come down to us!

Dear Queen Qiao I love you so much.

The concluding lines of a "Welcoming Song":

One more day I keep her here,

would it raise a fuss up there?

Two more days I keep her here,

---

① *Jin*, a traditional Chinese weight unit. 2 *jin* is equal to 1 kilo.

七夕文化透视 ▶▶▶
The Cowherd and the Weaver Fairy
A Study on the Folk Story and Double Seventh Day

would her thoughts drift away up there?
Three more days I keep her here,
would her family await her in tears?

Dear Queen Qiao, dear Queen Qiao,
though reluctant I have to see you off.

The following one is collected from the Zhangjia Chuan Autonomous County of Hui nationality, Tianshui city:

Dear Queen Qiao, dear Queen Qiao,
how she's pretty and how she's skillful!
Come down to us in a bunch of light,
I will serve you with all my heart.
Delicacies ready and soups served,
Queen Qiao is seated where girls swarmed.
Cowherd is sitting in the farthest corner,
where he is all alone, like a sneaky stalker.

With a bow low I ask for the tips,
for putting constant smiles on my in-laws' lips.
With flowers and fruits I ask for the tricks,
to keep my own will and way, whatever it takes.

To dear Queen Qiao I offer big eggs,
in seeking of stunning embroidery techs.
To dear Queen Qiao I offer juicy pears,
in a wish of going to see the world on mares.

The rebellious spirits of women in feudal society are quite obvious here. Some age-old Qiqiao songs enjoy great popularity, though vary in details more or less from place to place. The last song quoted above also circulates in Qingshui county, but the lines under "Cowherd is sitting in the farthest corner" are different. They go like this in that version:

> Breeze swirls up the yellow leaves,
> but dumps to the ground the dead broken twigs;
> With crystal water and silver bowl
> I rinse the pretty face of dear Queen Qiao.
>
> Her face is so pretty and her face so fair,
> on embroidery she has so much to share.
> To her I offer the sweetest melon,
> so that I'm granted with the prettiest pattern.
>
> To her I serve the tastiest peach,
> to acquire the sewing skills she's to teach.
> To her I make the most comfortable shoes,
> in a wish she will make me a sweetie as she is.

In addition to those traditional ones, there are regional additions of self-composed songs based on local means of production, the way of life, the folk customs and historical events. This is a proof that before the 1940s, the Qiqiao celebrations in those areas were grand events, too, but since most of them are located in transportation or economic hubs, the constant cultural fusion with the outside world finally shoved out the existence of some age-old traditions there.

七夕文化透视 ▸▸▸
The Cowherd and the Weaver Fairy
A Study on the Folk Story and Double Seventh Day

From the discussions above, we can see that the Weaver Fairy was transformed from Nüxiu, the female ancestor of the Qin people, and that the folk stories featuring the Weaver Fairy are closely related to Longnan (the South of Gansu) as well as Tianshui. At the same time, the speculation on Shujun, the remote ancestor of Zhou tribe, as the prototype for the Cowherd is supported by records scattered through different sections of *The Classics of Mountains and Seas*. In the east of Gansu, you may find many cultural and festive legacies concerning tillage, cultivation and farm cattle.

Tianshui city is located between the south and the east of Gansu province. Before the administrative adjustment of this area in which Wudu district was renamed to Longnan district, Longnan was a general name for the wide area including Wudu and Tianshui. This justifies the naming of a renowned academy in Tianshui as "Longnan Academy" as well as that of a local newspaper as "Longnan Times". But now after the administrative redivision, we have to differentiate between the two terms in use. During the times of Three Kingdoms, an independent administrative division prefecture Qin, was once set up in Tianshui area. The following dynasties, such as Tang, Song, Ming and Qing, followed suit. The time when Tianshui came by its name has always been believed to be (based on some historical records) during the reign of Emperor Wu of the Han Dynasty, to be exact, in the third year of Yuanding period (114 B.C.). But that is quite misleading. In fact, the name "Tianshui" originated in pre-Qin times instead of the Han Dynasty.

In late 1972, another big batch of cultural relics was unearthed from the ancient Qin tombs in Mengzhang village of Lixian county among which there was a horse-shaped bronze tripod. The scriptures

on its lid and belly read like this:

> Tianshui horse-shaped bronze tripod, weighs 9.5 kilos, with a capacity of 3 liters.

The bronze tripod is now on display at Lixian Museum. In the summer of 1996, another bronze tripod was unearthed around the town of Yan'guan located less than 10 kilometers to the east of Mengzhang village. The scriptures on the tripod[1] read: "Belongs to a Tianshui family." In the autumn of 1997, still another bronze tripod was unearthed in town Qishan which is still nearer to Mengzhang villiage and is engraved with the words: "Tianshui"[2]. In recent years, another bronze tripod was unearthed in Wenjia village located for 1 to 2 kilometers away from Mengzhang village. On its lid, it was carved: "The Tianshui horse-shaped bronze tripod weighs 9.5 kilos, with a capacity of 3 liters." According to "An Introduction to Official Posts" in *The Book of the Han Dynasty* (*Hanshu*,《汉书·百官志》): "Taipu is an official position in the Qin Dynasty. It was assisted by two officials who ran affairs with a staff consisting of Dajiu (大厩), Weiyang (未央) and Horse Clerk (家马) ... Horse Clerk was changed to Dongma (挏马 , meaning brewing wine with horse milk) in the first Taichu year under the reign of Emperor Wu of the Han Dynasty."

From this we can see that Horse Clerk was originally an official post in the Qin Dynasty whose duty was to take care of imperial horses. Considering the fact that the Han Dynasty kept many institutions from the Qin Dynasty, three inferences could be made here: first, "Tianshui" most probably acquired its name before the Qin Dynasty; second, the area was

---

[1]　The tripod is lost now.

[2]　The tripod is lost now.

named by the ancestors of the Qin people; third, Tianshui referred to only a small area including Yongxing, Yan'guan and Qishan which covered the now northeastern part of Lixian county. Possibly, it even spanned the area stretching from northeastern Lixian county to Tianshui town and the Queen's Terrace (娘娘坝) which stands in the current Qin district of Tianshui city, and reached the north of Xihe county from the south.

Naturally, the name "Tianshui" means "the fountainhead of the Celestial River, i.e., the Milky Way". The result of extensive literature research and archaeological discoveries has revealed that Tianshui city is where the Han River (the mother river of the now West Han River and the East Han River) originated. When Qin people migrated eastward to new habitat, they were accustomed to naming the mountains and rivers after what they had been familiar with in their old territory.

In conclusion, let me reiterate the main points in this section:

The ancestors of Qin people inhabited the area around the upper branch of the Han River. They then named the bright silvery Milky Way which played an important role in their daily lives as the Celestial Han River to correspond to the river on the ground. With the increasingly deepened cultural fusion between Zhou and Qin tribes, "Han" became "Cloudy Han" or "Celestial Han" which means "the River in the sky" when referring to the Milky Way. Qin people, in an effort to honor their remote ancestor Nüxiu who was famous for "weaving", named a star complex that consists of one big star and two tiny ones "the Weaver Fairy star", a name that was extensively used later. "Tianshui" (meaning the River in the sky, or the source of the River in the sky) is a name that came into use much later, but still during pre-Qin times when "Han" was popularly used as a word referring to "the celestial river" and "the great river which nurtured Qin people and fostered Qin culture before their eastward migration".

Chapter II
Ceremonious Qiqiao Customs Observed in Xihe and Lixian Counties

The earliest account of Qiqiao customs can be found in *A Miscellaneous Work from Chang'an* compiled by Ge Hong, as was mentioned above. Another reference could be found in *A Handbook and Calendar for Farming* (*Simin Yueling*,《四民月令》) by Cui Shi (崔寔) of the Eastern Han Dynasty. Here is the description:

> (On the 7th of July,) People prepare food for journeys, pick cocklebur fruits, drink and eat delicacies, scatter fragrant powder in the courtyard and pray for blessings from the Cowherd and the Weaver Fairy.

Zhou Chu (236-297), a scholar who lived and wrote at the beginning of the Western Jin Dynasty, recorded in his *The Records of Regional Folk Customs* (*Fengtu Ji*,《风土记》):

> On July 7th, the courtyard is swept clean and a feast arranged there. Drinks and delicacies are served and fragrant powder is scattered. Then, girls express their goodwill during a meeting between the Cowherd and the Weaver Fairy stars. The worshippers (and the celebrants at the same time) keep their

七夕文化透视 ▸▸▸
The Cowherd and the Weaver Fairy
A Study on the Folk Story and Double Seventh Day

secret wishes to themselves, staying up late in the courtyard praying. If lucky enough, they may catch a glimpse of steaming white cloud and frost around the Milky Way sparkling with colorful glares. That is regarded as an auspicious omen.

Zong Lin of the Southern Dynasties wrote in his *Festivals and Folk Customs of the Jing and Chu Area* (*Jingchu Suishi Ji*,《荆楚岁时记》):

> On the evening, girls in every family twist silk threads of five colors in strands, threading 7 needle of gold, silver and valuable stones, serve melons and fruits on the desks in the courtyard to pray for good luck, happiness and superior needlework skills.

Figure 10   Praying for Good Luck Through Different Activities
by Lu Haiyan

Numerous literary works written after the Han and Wei Dynasties depict a similar scene of Double Seventh Day celebration. As far as I know, the Qiqiao customs observed and celebrations conducted in Xihe and Lixian counties are the grandest and the longest-lasting with the most particular forms and procedures. For girls in these two counties, Double Seventh Day is a far more important and joyful festival in comparison with the Spring Festival. In recent years, the festival has not been celebrated as grandly as it used to be in the central towns, but is still so in rural areas as a time-honored tradition handed down from our ancestors.

Approaching the end of June each year, the village girls of Xihe and Lixian counties in the south of Gansu province convene to prepare for the upcoming Double Seventh Day. Each praying site usually consists of twenty to thirty girls residing in neighbouring areas, each contributing to the occasion in her own way. Those who can afford money donate, those who can spare utilities will provide for festive activities, while others who can spare time take on more preparation work. The girls put their heads together to compose new verses for the year. The key point is to decide in whose home Queen Qiao will be invited to stay during the celebration. Usually the household with spacious rooms and a courtyard belonging to an unmarried girl blessed with open-minded parents will be preferred.

七夕文化透视 ▶▶▶
The Cowherd and the Weaver Fairy
A Study on the Folk Story and Double Seventh Day

Figure 11 Qiqiao Rites (1)

by Lu Haiyan

On the last day of lunar June, the girls from both urban and rural areas will go to the shops selling paper artifacts to "escort Queen Qiao home". The shops which have had a lot of paper models of Queen Qiao[1] ready beforehand have big money to make on this day. Standing at least 1 meter tall, the paper model dressed in bright-colored blouse and beautifully embroidered shoes will be respectably seated on a desk in a decorated room when escorted home. With incense burning and candles lighted up, the girls let off firecrackers at the gate to welcome Queen Qiao. In the evening, the girls pray through singing and dancing for the descent of Queen Qiao from Heaven to the mortal world in front of the desk where her model is seated. At the welcoming rites during the day, the verses chanted are usually traditional ones like the following:

[1]   The face of the model is painted on a layer of white paper which is lined with layers of hemp paper having been dried on a mould of a human face.

On July 1st the Gate to Heaven is Thrown Open

On July 1st the Gate to Heaven is thrown open,
I have asked Queen Qiao to descend so often.
Queen Qiao, do Come! Ride on a piece of cloud,
and I will welcome you aloud;
Queen Qiao, in flowery embroidered shoes
along the Milky Way she goes.

When she finally comes,
cooking skills Queen Qiao will teach.
Reading and writing will also be a matter of ease.
Down to the lotus seat I invite her to settle,
then at her shoe-embroidery skill I admire and marvel.

In front of her altar the yellow candle is burning,
how to embroider beautiful plums I'm learning.
Tea and snacks I serve in awe,
a pair of deft hands for me she has in store.

Yummy cakes I prepared with all my heart,
for her effort in turning me deft and smart.
See you off and see you in,
every year you are my source of well-being!

Figure 12 Qiqiao Dancing

by Lu Haiyan

In the following days leading up to lunar July 7th, the room will be filled day and night with girl celebrants, including girls from other villages or neighborhoods. Squads of girls swing their arms singing and dancing while holding hands together. Among the newly composed verses, there are also traditional ones passed down from their predecessors of who-knows-how-many generations. Take the following one as an example:

Early spring earth freezes so hard,
as the winter chill plays its full part.
Earth in February starts to melt,
with the fish's desire for sky felt.
March enwrapes hills with pink peach blossoms,
while April is dotted with willow groves so prosperous.

The Double Fifth Festival[①] falls in May,
finds the rice wine of realgar served in tray.
June awes at the ripening yellow field of wheat,
while July decorates the courtyard grapevines with fruits sweet.

August entertains us with melon pieces like a crest,
and buckwheat in September is stored in wooden chest.
October lights up streets with red lanterns of persimmon,
while snowflakes in November swirl in air like hurricane.

① The Double Fifth Festival is more popularly known as the Dragon Boat Festival in southern China where it is traditionally celebrated with boat competitions. But for Xihe and Lixian counties of Gansu province in northwestern China where water resources are not as rich, boat competitions are not part of the local custom. That's why we use the term "the Double Fifth Festival" instead.

七夕文化透视 ▸▸▸
The Cowherd and the Weaver Fairy
A Study on the Folk Story and Double Seventh Day

> December lures people out for Spring Festival shopping,
> when streets and roads filled with people happily talking.
> Queen Qiao my lady, come down to us as fast as you may.
> I have a year-round story to share and many a word to say!

The climatic changes around the year, as well as the corresponding changes in people's working and living schedule, are described here, reflecting people's concern about the climate and the attempt to pass down their agricultural knowledge and life experience to the next generation. Some other verses provide historical and cultural knowledge, or in some cases, common sense useful in daily lives which serve an obvious function of knowledge transmission.

In addition to the traditional ones, new Qiqiao songs are composed every year, of which most are closely related to social reality, aiming to express the celebrants' feelings and emotions through rich metaphors or analogies. Sometimes, girls will invite female elders to act as their mentors in suggestion-giving and preparation work, but the latter will not be allowed participation in welcoming and seeing-off rites, as well as singing and dancing activities during the celebration. Once devoted celebrants themselves, the married women are more than willing to lend a hand, more or less as a tribute to their lost youth and flowery years. Since the 1950s, girls have started to ask for help in verse composition from local intellectuals and educated youth, but the best lines, which are saturated with girls' true emotions and deepest understanding of their lives, still turn out to be from under their own pens. Cited below are lines from old times before the Liberation:

> Opium rare, opium dear,
> one silver coin a small puff mere.

Blown in and blown out,
white puffs weaken a man once so stout.

In fits of streaming tears and nose,
everything's traded for a dose.
With sons and daughters sold in a row,
nothing left was tradable any more.

My dear father and my dear husband,
do bid your farewell to Opium for good.

Drama stage being set up under a tree,
is an invitation to a performance put on for free.
I hurry my steps to invite my sister along,
to free her from the sighs and frown.

But she was so sad as not to come along,
as her life is so miserably forlorn.
With farmland sold and furniture gone,
her husband resumes gambling in town.

Once again penniless at dawn
He comes back home for more stuff to pawn.
Having nothing to eat and no mood for drink,
no way out she sees in heartache.

She can do nothing but blame her parents,
for all the pains, tears and desperate moments.
All the cares they shown on her marital well-being,
were so easily brushed aside by some monetary real thing.

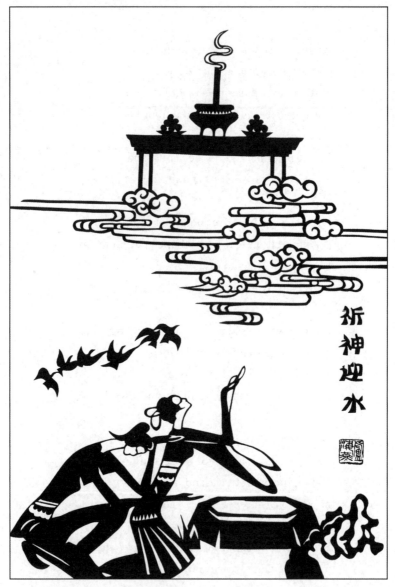

Figure 13 Water–fetching Rite

by Lu Haiyan

The criticism against mercenary marriage is too sharp and direct to be ignored here. Some long verses can be chanted for more than ten minutes before coming to an end.

"Xing Qing", the visits, or to be more exact, the artistic exchanges between praying sites of different villages and neighborhoods by squads of girls, start from the 3rd or 4th of lunar July. These enrich the girl's compositional experience while serving as an occasion of socialization.

The morning of lunar July 7th witnesses the water-fetching rite in which girls rise early for a trip to clear springs for the first bucket of water in the morning. In the evening, all the girls gather together in the room where Queen Qiao is worshiped, bringing along a strand of kidney bean sprouts, a small bowl or a basin. The bean sprouts are then put into the basin filled with spring water which they fetched in the morning, and the shadows cast on the bottom of the basin are closely observed for deciphering. If it is too crowded indoors, some girls will go outside with a candle, trying their best to read the secret messages from Queen Qiao. This activity called "Bu Qiao" (卜巧 , decoding messages hidden in the shadows cast by bean sprouts to make predictions on whether you will be blessed with a good marriage, deftness or wisdom or not) is conducted from the beginning to the end with the accompaniment of Qiqiao songs. Take the following song as an example:

> Making a wish in front of Queen Qiao,
> I pray for desirable shadow and shape in my bowl.
> The image of delicate flowers betoken me as smart,
> while that of a shabby fan poses me as a slut.

七夕文化透视 ▶▶▶
The Cowherd and the Weaver Fairy
A Study on the Folk Story and Double Seventh Day

Those of needles promise me with dexterity,

while that of an iron nail allows no chance for like capacity.

Those of slim silk threads a token of good skill,

while that of a coarse cord calls for more practice still.

The shape of nice scissors poses me as a good tailor,

while that of a crude trowel an expertise seeker.

The shape of a rolling pin is what I want,

instead of that of a clumsy dog-punch rod.

Do bless me with the shadow of a writing brush,

as that of a featherless chicken will drive me nuts.

The shape of an ink holder promises me with intelligence,

while a bucket a token of toil on long distance.

Do bless me with pattern desirable!

You may find me a worshipper reliable.

Do bless me with the shape I crave!

Toward the future I will be so brave.

And there is another example:

Bean sprouts tiny and curve,

Queen Qiao I devotedly serve.

Neither jewelry nor silver do I want,

only a nice mother-in-law of whom I'm fond,

plus a good husband hard to find near or yond.

In both songs, girls' benign expectations of their future marital life are expressed when they try to decode the messages believed to be given by Queen Qiao. This is a rare chance for girls to express their true feelings and desires for happiness in a roundabout way under the strict moral shackles of feudalism.

The evening of lunar July 7th, also the last evening of the celebration which has already lasted for 7 days, brings the event to its climax with girls singing and dancing most vigorously. As this grand ceremony approaches its end, elder girls, who are scared of the prospect of soon being married off to a total stranger in a totally strange family without any hope of participation in such a celebration with their dear friends, perform the rites even more devotedly in an atmosphere tinted with departing sorrows. In the depths of the night, girls escort the model of Queen Qiao to the nearest riverbank and burn it there to the accompaniment of farewell songs. In the past, some girls were so absorbed in the sorrows of departure during overnight singing and dancing that they got swollen eyes the following day. That was their particular way to vent out their anger against the overwhelming pressure from feudal ethics. For those married assistants, usually young wives, the once-a-year opportunity for mutual learning and free venting of personal emotions is also an occasion that brings back the memories of their younger times. One of the Seeing-off Qiqiao songs usually sung on the evening of lunar July 7th goes like this:

七夕文化透视 ▶▶▶
The Cowherd and the Weaver Fairy
A Study on the Folk Story and Double Seventh Day

July 7th Sees the End of the Festival

July 7th is the last day
when to Queen Qiao I have to say goodbye.
I want to keep her here for one day or more,
lest she could not find the way back as before.

I want to keep her here for two days or more,
Lest at the Southern Gate[①] she would be left outdoor.
I want to keep her here for three days or more,
lest the Jade Emperor call me names in angry roar.

The ink characters under my writing-brush tip,
record the 7 days' happiness I recall in weep.
Wiping off tears time and again from my face,
there's still a lot you spare no time to teach.

Helpless and sad, I drag my feet
to see you off at the gate.
Brother magpie, brother magpie,
would you carry her onto the sky
on the white cloud, under a yellow canopy,
escort her safe and sound across the Milky Way.

---

① According to Chinese fairy tales, it is the gate to Heaven.

In the verses quoted above, the Jade Emperor is believed to be the father of the Weaver Fairy, the man who has the final say in her marriage and lifelong happiness. They identify themselves with the Weaver Fairy in a shared fate of having no say in their lives. The rite of escorting Queen Qiao to the riverside for the farewell rite suggests a faint connection with the old folk story featured by a river in the sky, the Milky Way.

Girls' fear for loss (of their youth, friends, happiness and carefree moments) on the last evening is vividly described in one of the songs:

> In colorful dress and beautiful shoes,
> Queen Qiao is seen off in beaded tears.
> Following her out of the door then gate,
> I can hardlly drag my feet.
>
> Happy moments are short and rare,
> making the rest of time hard to bear.
> Out of sight she's finally gone,
> leaving behind her a girl so forlorn.
>
> Out of sight she finally disappears.
> leaving behind her a girl in tears.

The age-old Qiqiao customs which are popular in Xihe and Lixian counties are observed in some other adjoining counties such as Tianshui Town of Qinchen district under the jurisdiction of

七夕文化透视 ▸▸▸
The Cowherd and the Weaver Fairy
A Study on the Folk Story and Double Seventh Day

Tianshui city, but only on a reduced scale and with less grandeur. There are no beautiful paper models of Queen Qiao and no rhythmic foot-stamping to singing, which especially highlight the particular splendor of the ceremony in Xihe and Lixian counties. Taking the above discussion into consideration, the ceremonious celebrations conducted in Xihe and Lixian are most probably a reflection of the aborigines' collective subconsciousness inherited from their ancestors which deserves further study.

Chapter III

A Study on the Folk Story, the Cow Culture and the Qiqiao Customs Popular in Eastern Gansu and Shaanxi Provinces

Section 1 The Geographical Names, Temples and Customs in Eastern Gansu and the Central Area of Shaanxi Province

As for the belief that the basin of the Malian River in Qingyang city, Gansu province, was the fountainhead of Zhou culture where Zhou people conceived the image of Cowherd after their ancestor Shujun, we can find abundant proof in eastern Gansu province and the central area of Shaanxi province, among which there are numerous geographical names and cow-related customs.

In Linyou, a county of Baoji city, Shaanxi province, there is a Temple of the Weaver Fairy and a Tomb of the Cowherd built a long time ago. There is also a Crouching-Cow mountain and a Crouching-cow cave. All these relics are related to the cow of magical power in the folk story "The Cowherd and the Weaver Fairy". In Volume 1 of *The Renewed County Annals of Linyou* (《麟游县新志》), you may find the following record:

> The bizarre shape gives the Crouching-Cow mountain to the west of Mountain Qinglian its name. With its front

Chapter III
A Study on the Folk Story, the Cow Culture and the Qiqiao Customs
Popular in Eastern Gansu and Shaanxi Provinces | 061

bulging like a cow head and shoulders, and with the back sloping down like a cow crouching on the ground, the mountain does look like a crouching cow. A cave on it was thus called Crouching-Cow Cave.

Both the mountain and the cave play a part in the local version of the story "The Cowherd and the Weaver Fairy".

According to *A Study on Temples and Ancestral Halls of Xi'an* (《西安府祠庙考》) in volume 504 of *An Extensive Collection of Literature of All Times* (*Gujin Tushu Jicheng*,《古今图书集成》), in Wugong county of Xianyang city where the Zhou people inhabited in early times, there was a Temple of Magical Stone Cow sitting on "the Cow Mountain" in the west, suggesting an obvious connection with the folk story. About 5.5 kilometers to the west of Wugong county, there is another mountain named "Stone-cow mountain", with yet another called "Cow-herding Mountain" to the southeast (for reference, please refer to volume 495 of *An Extensive Collection of Literature of All Times*).

In Yongshou county to the east of Bin county of Xianyang city, there was once a temple dedicated to the magical stone cow on a Stone-Cow Mountain, too. In volume 1 of *The County Annals of Yongshou* (《永寿县志》) printed in 1888, an item reads:

> According to the old version of the county annals, a Stone-Cow mountain rested 5 kilometers to the west of the county. There was a Temple of Magical Stone-Cow on it.

In volume 2, another similar item reads as follows:

> The temple of Magical Stone Cow is located on Stone-cow mountain, which is 5 kilometers away to the west of the county.

In the same volume, another sentence reads:

> Queen Qiao's Temple lies on Chenjia mountain which is 7.5 kilometers to the east of the county.

In volume 4, there is a brief introduction to local customs:

> On the previous day of the Beginning of Spring (立春), it's a tradition for officials to welcome the coming of Spring on the eastern outskirts. Constables put on colorful costumes of opera performances. Instrumental ensembles are organized and colorful flags are planted all around the venue. Everywhere, you can see people beaming in festive glee. On Double Seventh Day, young girls offer sacrifices of various fruits and bean sprouts to pray for blessings from the Weaver Fairy, the goddess.

In Gansu and Shaanxi, a folk name for "the Weaver Fairy, the goddess" (the term used by intellectuals) is Queen Qiao. For local people, this immortalized figure makes a good match for the Cow God, who is worshiped in the local Temple of the Magical Stone Cow.

The most particular customs in eastern Gansu and the central area of Shaanxi province are the ones connected with tillage culture, among which some look like in want of a direct connection with the folk story, but suggest an indirect connection which provide

Chapter III
A Study on the Folk Story, the Cow Culture and the Qiqiao Customs
Popular in Eastern Gansu and Shaanxi Provinces | 063

七夕文化透视 ▸▸▸
The Cowherd and the Weaver Fairy
A Study on the Folk Story and Double Seventh Day

appropriate cultural environment or hotbed for the breeding and growth of it, as well as perpetuation and establishment of rituals associated with it in the local culture. About the tillage-related customs in the east of Gansu province, a paragraph from volume 5 of *The Prefecture Annals of Jingning* (《静宁州志》) compiled during Kangxi years of the Qing Dynasty provides some evdence:

> Every year, on the previous day of the Beginning of Spring, the God of Agriculture is worshiped on the eastern outskirts, and officials line up to conduct the Spring-welcome ritual. On the day of Beginning of Spring, there is a ritual of offering sacrifices to the God of Revitalization (勾芒神). Then a Spring-urging ritual (鞭春礼) is conducted at the eastern gate of the city where the prefecture is based.

In volume 10 of *The County Annals of Zhuanglang* (《庄浪县志》) compiled in 1769, there is another item with more detailed descriptions:

> On the previous day of the Beginning of Spring, "Farm-cattle Welcoming" ritual is conducted. Local operas and costume dances are performed to welcome the God of Revitalization into the city. People gather to enjoy a jolly time. It's common practice on this day to eat spring rolls and go on spring outings with family and friends.

A still more detailed account can be found in volume 3 of *The County Annals of Qiangyang* (《庆阳县志》) compiled in 1934:

> During the Qing Dynasty, it was an established custom

for local officials to welcome the coming of Spring on eastern outskirts of the county on the previous day of the Beginning of Spring. A paper model of a so-called "Spring Cow" was erected beforehand. Streets and neighborhoods were decorated with colorful flags and paraded with musical bands. Juggling, along with other kinds of performances, were offered. Town people, no matter young or old, women or men, would all go out to enjoy the lively scene. This event was called "Urging the spring cow (to work hard)". When the ritual was done, people would dash forward for a handful of scraps of "Spring Cow" to take home. If someone successfully grabbed some bits from the paper model and tucked them under the cattle trough in his house, it was believed that he would be blessed with safety and prosperity in the upcoming year. Spring rolls were traditional food for the Beginning of Spring. Though the shift of the day into the Beginning of Spring occured at midnight, people kept the custom of staying up late in a hope of warding off typical drowsiness often felt in the spring time. According to *The Almanac*, it's an auspicious day fit for wedding ceremonies.

A excerpt from "The Preface to Local Festivals and Customs" in *A Renewed Edition of County Annals of Lingtai* (《重修灵台县志·风俗节序》) reads like this:

According to local customs, on the previous day of the Beginning of Spring, the county magistrate would call for a convention of local people from all walks of life, including practitioners from 72 different businesses. They were put into

Chapter III
A Study on the Folk Story, the Cow Culture and the Qiqiao Customs
Popular in Eastern Gansu and Shaanxi Provinces 065

七夕文化透视 ▸▸▸
The Cowherd and the Weaver Fairy
A Study on the Folk Story and Double Seventh Day

different groups, each wearing red coats, black trousers and facial make-up featuring different stories. They dressed up and convened at the local administrative building for an inspection which if they passed, would allow them to participate in a "Shehuo performance" in public. On the morning of the following day, headed by the county magistrate and his staff in official robes, the performers and townspeople all congregated on the eastern outskirts to welcome the coming of Spring. The model of Goumang, the God of Revitalization, was erected on the left, while a colorful model of the spring cow would be displayed on the right. Essays eulogizing the arrival of Spring would be showcased on both sides. Under the guidance of the local courtesy official, all those present would participate in a ritual of three kneeling-downs and nine kowtows. Then, the God of Cultivation would be escorted to his designated position out of the city gate. As the last moment ticking into the day of the Beginning of Spring, everyone would repeat the ritual of three kneeling-downs and nine kowtows, followed by the issuance of congratulatory messages. At the same time, colorful papers would be knitted into strips to make a huge cow. This was called "Urging the Spring Cow". People from near and far crowded there, all eager to compete for a handful of spring cow scraps as they believed it would bring them good luck in the upcoming year.

This custom is observed in parts of Shaanxi province, too, which in some cases is quite similar to practices in eastern Gansu. In "Folk Customs" (《风俗》) appended to *The County Annals of Gaoling* (《高陵县志·礼仪抄略》) compiled in the year 1542, there is a similar record:

The Spring-urging Ritual involves building an earthen model of cow on the eastern outskirts, while a model of the God of Revitalization is erected in the Temple of the God of Earth (后土宫) according to the local custom. On the day preceding the Beginning of Spring, the county magistrate and his staff, all dressed up in their official robes, go to the outskirts to welcome the Spring accompanied by music and opera performances as per local traditions. Each official engaged in the event should wear a flower on his official cap. After having escored the Model of Spring Cow to the Temple of the God of Earth, they put it beside Goumang, the God of Revitalization, in the front hall. On the day of the Beginning of Spring, delicacies, wines, fruits and candles are served in front of the God of Revitalization, while the officials kowtow four times in the accompaniment of music. The county magistrate steps forward, kneels down again, and offers wine three times, then bends forward to kowtow four more times along with all the other officials. Afterwards, the officials line up beside the cow. The county magistrate beats the big drum three times, and the officials take turns beating the cow three times until the earthen model falls down in pieces. Congratulatory messages are recited: "... [W]e offer the earthen cow to pay our respects to Spring."

A similar account in *The County Annals of Lintong* (《临潼县志》) suggests the possibility that this was an established folk custom even before the Ming Dynasty.

As late as dozens of years ago, the "Spring-urging ritual" remained an important festival in Ningxian county, Gansu province.

Chapter III
A Study on the Folk Story, the Cow Culture and the Qiqiao Customs
Popular in Eastern Gansu and Shaanxi Provinces   067

七夕文化透视 ▸▸▸
The Cowherd and the Weaver Fairy
A Study on the Folk Story and Double Seventh Day

On the Beginning of Spring, a cow-shaped structure made of wooden planks and strips standing around 6.5 meters high and 10 meters wide was erected on the eastern outskirts. It was covered with reed mats first, then plastered with hemp paper, and yellow paper last to resemble its skin on which certain patterns were painted to mimic the real thing. This is known as the Spring Cow. The county magistrate, followed by other officials and local gentries, feigned to whip the cow to ensure a good beginning for spring cultivation. This ritual was recorded as a local custom in many places, but such a large cow model used in such a festive way was a rare scene not found elsewhere.

As we have discussed above, in contrast to the folklore, Goumang, the God of Revitalization, replaced the Cowherd and the Weaver Fairy in official sacrifices, as the intellectuals have a strong faith in *The Book of Rites*. In the Section "The Lunar Months" (《礼记·月令》) of the book, it says, "The god in charge (on the Beginning of Spring) is Taogao, with Goumang, the God of Revitalization, as his assistant." "On the Beginning of Spring, the emperor heads a squad of kings, ministers, aristocrats and officials to welcome Spring on the eastern outskirts of the capital." But these official formalities have little to do with folk customs. According to the account regarding Spring sacrifice in *The Book of Rites*, there is no mention of spring cows or the "Spring-Cow-Urging ritual" conducted by whipping the cow model. In volume 6 of *Records of Folk Customs in Kaifeng the East Capital* (*Dongjing Menghua Lu*, 《东京梦华录》) written during the Song Dynasty, there is an account of "Spring-urging ritual" practiced during the Northern Song Dynasty, but only as a symbolic etiquette, not a festival celebrated by the whole society like in eastern Gansu. The ritual conducted in eastern Gansu and Shaanxi province on the day before the Beginning

of Spring is actually a combination of ancient spring rituals and folk stories featuring the magical cow and the Cowherd.

There are also some geographical names concerning cows in eastern Gansu province. In "The Greographical Conditions I" from *The Renewed Edition of County Annals of Zhenyuan*, You may read the following descriptions:

> The Crouching-Cow mountain lies about 35 kilometers west of the town. Standing on an vast expanse of towering highlands, it looks like a crouching cow, with its head, mouth, ears and horns complete and vivid. The eye-shaped hill is located where the eyes are supposed to be, as if it's looking back at the moon. On the front slope of the highlands, some hoof prints are discernible, which, as the natives would tell you, were left when the cow went down to the river for drinking.

What deserves our special attention are the folk customs related to cows in eastern Gansu, where a custom of "Cow-alarming ceremony" is still practiced on the first day of lunar New Year. In the book *The Folk Customs of Eastern Gansu Province* (《陇东风俗》), there is an account of this ceremony:

> In some places of eastern Gansu province, there is a festival called "Cow-alarming" dedicated to cows on the first day of the lunar New Year. To awaken cows from their winter idleness and prepare them for the upcoming busy farming season, farmers release cows and oxen from their bullpens to roam freely in wildness and uncultivated fields for the whole day...

Chapter III
A Study on the Folk Story, the Cow Culture and the Qiqiao Customs
Popular in Eastern Gansu and Shaanxi Provinces | 069

七夕文化透视 ▶▶▶
The Cowherd and the Weaver Fairy
A Study on the Folk Story and Double Seventh Day

Early in the morning, young lads who have finished their breakfast of noodles joyfully let their cow or ox out for a elaborate decoration with red silk cloth and beautiful flowers. Two strings of firecrackers will be hung dangling down from the animals' nostrils, which are ignited when everything is ready. The sudden burst of firecrackers set the shocked animals off in a vigorous dash. With their tails flying and hooves high in the air, the cows and oxen, reinless and load-free, swoosh out of gates and into the wilderness, putting on a spectacular scene of lively running competition. The bouncing animals enjoy themselves heartily in the spring field, while villagers standing around, applauding in ecouragement. The lethargy which has lingered over the village for the whole winter is instantly swept clean.

"The Cow-alarming ceremony" is also a good opportunity for young lads to show off their horsemanship and bravery. Tough young men would throw themselves onto the back of the animal before it dashes through the gate, while their family, neighbors and friends cheer them on. If some of them get thrown off onto the ground, they will get up quickly and give it another try. If the elders of the family, out of concern for their hard-working pal, forbid the young man to ride on it so that the animal can get a rest, they will offer him a donkey instead. Some younger kids in their imitation of their elder brothers but unable to mount a cow, will ride on some big sheep with firecrackers dangling from their noses too! What a sight it is when troops of cows, oxen, sheep and donkeys run wild in the field amidst the thunderous crackling of firecrackers.

On the evening of lunar January 15th, neighbors exchange lamps made of flour. This tradition is called "seeing cow off". According to tradition, stealing flour lamp known as "cow-stealing" is allowed, too. From this we can see that cows or oxen play a key role in the social life of eastern Gansu where agriculture is the primary livelihood for local people. How well a family will fare in the new year depends mostly on the work of their cows or oxen. One of the most popular practices in eastern Gansu is naming male newborns as "Niuwa" (baby cow) or "Niuwa ge" (cow brother).

On the second day of lunar February, people in eastern Gansu keep a tradition of paying respect to the bullpen before the first ploughing of their farmland in the new year. The whole family kneel down in the bullpen, lights strings of firecrackers, burns fragrant incense and kowtows several times to pray for favorable weather and a good harvest. On this day, even if you do not plough your field, you are supposed to harness your cow or ox and plough the field for at least one circle. Then, scatter some grain seeds in the soil and fertilize the patch to simulate the act of tilling. From these customs we can see the importance the local people attach to and the idolization of cows.

In the area surrounding Pingliang city in eastern Gansu, the practice of trying the plough (试犁) at the beginning of a new year is called "Cow-starting" (开牛). Before the start of spring tillage, villagers choose an auspicious day to test their plough. Once the day is determined, the direction from which the God of Happiness is supposed to descend can also be decided, based on the direction of the opening of a particular magpie nest. The organizer harnesses his cow to the yoke ploughs in front of a big applauding audience. If the plough, ploughshare and reins all stay solid and in good condition, favorable weather, a good harvest and a prosperous year

Chapter III
A Study on the Folk Story, the Cow Culture and the Qiqiao Customs
Popular in Eastern Gansu and Shaanxi Provinces

071

七夕文化透视 ▸▸▸
The Cowherd and the Weaver Fairy
A Study on the Folk Story and Double Seventh Day

can be expected. Even today, some elderly farmers steadfastly stick to this custom. The direction for the descent of the God of Happiness is determined by the direction of the opening in a magpie nest— this is another unique custom found nowhere else. It is most probably related to the folk story of "The Cowherd and the Weaver Fairy" in that magpies flock together to make a bridge for the couple's reunion over the Milky Way. Traditionally regarded as auspicious birds bringing good news to families, magpies always feature red paper cutting plastered onto window panes during the Spring Festival. The combination of cow, the only animal, and magpie, the only bird, in the "Cow-alarming" ritual is a very interesting cultural phenomenon.

Another long-standing tradition in the areas surrounding the Maliang River is the making of steamed buns stuffed with dates. The multi-layered buns about three centimeters thick are usually shared among the family and with the cow by the field as part of the sacrificial ritual dedicated to the God of the Earth.

Besides, it is a custom in eastern Gansu to refrain from working cows on certain days, including Double Seventh Day, Clear and Bright Day, Grain Rain Beginning and Double 5th Day (the Dragon Boat Festival). In some places, even the work of donkeys is forbidden on these days. Hence, there is an old saying: "Cows and donkeys work so hard, three days[1] off are fully justified."

From the discussions above, we can see that in eastern Gansu and Shaanxi where were once the early habitat of the Zhou people and the territories of the ancient states of Bin and Ta, people attach great importance to tillage and cow culture. None of these customs

---

[1] The three days include the Clear and Bright Day, the Grain Rain and the Double Fifth Festival.

have ever been observed in any other area. These customs show that the farmers who have lived in this area for generations have established very strong emotional bonds with their cows through year-round farming and tilling. Cows are not only regarded as family members, but also as magical beings. In my opinion, this is the fittest soil to breed the folk story of the Cowherd and the a magical cow.

By the way, I'd like to discuss the history of "God of Cow King". The earliest mention of the title "Cow King" occurs in volume 3 of *The Notes by Riverside in Spring* (*Chunzhu Jiwen*,《春渚纪闻》) by He Yuan of the Northern Song Dynasty. It describes a man who dreamed of being chased to a place where, "Upon looking up, he found a inscribed board with four golden characters 'Palace of Cow King'. When he entered the palace, he ran into his late aunt who stared at him in shock and told him: 'I was fond of beef and got numerous cows killed in my past life. That's why I am detained here, enduring endless misery. What's especially unbearable is my meal—3 *jin* of it a day! At that moment, a cow-headed man came and brought her a bowl of iron thorns." The purpose of this short story seems to discourage the killing of cows and oxen rather than depicting the ruler of the Palace of Cow King. Another example comes from *Shuofu* (《说郛》), a quotation from *Pedantic Conversations from a Living Room* (*Xishang Futan*,《席上腐谈》) by Yu Yan reads: "Someone from the Central Plains said there is a temple of Cow King in the North where hundreds of cows and oxen are painted on the wall, with the Cow King seated in the middle. You know what? The Cow King turns out to be Ran Boniu (冉伯牛), the pupil of Confucius!" Puchen city where the author lived during the Song Dynasty is now Puchen county in Fujian province. Worshiping Ran Boniu, the pupil of Confucius, as the Cow King must

Chapter III
A Study on the Folk Story, the Cow Culture and the Qiqiao Customs
Popular in Eastern Gansu and Shaanxi Provinces | 073

have resulted from the misconception of dilettante intellectuals in the South who mistakenly associated the Cow King in the Cow-King-worship ritual with the pupil of Confucius only because they found the character "cow" in his name. In "The Year-round Customs" in *A Book of Farmer's Calendar* (*Yueling Guangyi*, 《月令广义·岁令》) by Feng Yingjing of the Ming Dynasty, the author states: "People worship the Cow King to pay their respects to cows. However, in the South, there is an absurd practice of offering sacrifices to the portrait of Ran Boniu in this effort." A reasonable speculation is that the worship of the Cow King began even earlier, with the earliest records in "The History of the Qin Dynasty" from *Records of the Grand Historian*: about a Temple of the Giant Cow built in 739 B.C. In my opinion, the worship of the Cow King most probably initiated with the Zhou tribe, whose culture mixed with that of the Qin, prompting the latter to start building temples for the Cow King as well.

In China, the tradition of protecting and worshiping cows boasts of a long history. According to the section "On Rules and Principles" from *Records of the Grand Historian* (《史记·律书》):

> The Cowherd Star symbolizes Yang-qi (阳气), which stimulates the revitalization of everything from the frozen earth. Cows are connected with tillage and cultivation, which also bring plants out of the ground.

Here, the grand historian had already illustrated the name of "the Cowherd Star" from a perspective of seasonal shifts and the changes of Yin and Yang. This perpective encompasses not only the result of astronomic research, the study of calendars and Yin-Yang theory before the Western Han Dynasty, but also folk religion and practice.

A sentence from "On the Overwhelming Vital Principle of the Way" in *Huainan Zi* (《淮南子·说山》) goes like this:

> Even if the killing of an old and infirm cow can save that of a strong, speedy horse, do not do it. Cow killing is ominous as it heralds doom.

The footnotes added by Xu Shen read: "Cows till the earth to feed people with grain so that the whole country thrives. That's why cow killing is forbidden by law in every dynasty. Offenders will be sentenced to death as punishment." Another example comes from "A Satire against Extravagance" in *The New Preface* (《新序·刺奢》) in which King Mu of the kingdom Zou during the Warring States period once said: "The farmers till the land with their well-fed cows. They bend down to plant and cultivate while sweating all over." This tells us that the hard working farmers will not let their cows work unfed. All of these are solid proof for farmers' deep emotional bond with their working companions in ancient times.

From these examples we can see that the magical cow in "The Cowherd and the Weaver Fairy" is imbued with deep historical and cultural connotations and is built on the soil of fairy tales as well as religions of ancient times, which we should not neglect.

Section 2   The Qiqiao Customs Practiced in Eastern Gansu and the Central Area of Shaanxi Province

In "The Local Customs IV" (《风俗四》) of volume 32 in *The Prefecture Annals of Qingyang*, there is an item which reads like this:

Chapter III
A Study on the Folk Story, the Cow Culture and the Qiqiao Customs
Popular in Eastern Gansu and Shaanxi Provinces | 075

On the 7th of lunar July, girls pray for blessings from the Weaver Fairy. They serve fruits and melons on desks, throw bean sprouts they have grown into a bowl of water to foretell their fate by decoding the message hidden in the shadows cast on the bottom of the bowl.

This custom is practiced all over the Qingyang area. In *A Study on Folk Customs in Prefecture Pingliang* (《平凉府风俗考》) quoted in volume 553 of *An Extensive Collection of Literature of All Times*, you may find similar accounts. In the following literature which include "A Record of Folk Customs" (《乡土志》) in volume 4 of *The Prefecture Annals of Jingning* (《静宁州志》) recompiled during the reign of Emperor Kangxi, the section titled "Local Customs" (《风俗》) in volume 3 of *The Prefecture Annals of Jingning* recompiled in the 11th year under the reign of Emperor Qianlong, "Local Customs" in volume 10 of *The County Annals of Zhuanglang* hand-copied in the 34th year under the reign of Emperor Qianlong, "The Customs, Traditions and Festivals" (《民俗，风俗，岁时》) in volume 3 of *The County Annals of Qingyang*, and "The Local Nationalities" in *A Renewed Edition of the County Annals of Zhenyuan* (《重修镇原县志·民族志》), with the last two both recompiled during the years of the Republic of China, the description about the custom is quite sketchy, but an account from *The Folk Customs of Zhengning* (《正宁民俗》) offers us a glimpse into it:

On Double Seventh Day, local women conduct a series of interesting Qiqiao activities to honor the occassion. On lunar June 6th, a month before the festival, girls immerse the beans which have been carefully hand-picked into a bowl of

clear water and put it in some shady place. The water will be changed every two to three days till neat, plump bean sprouts of white and yellow colors have grown to around 3 inches long which will then be tied up with colorful silk threads into small bunches. The procedure will be repeated as the sprouts grow longer and longer. When they finally reach around 10 inches long, three to five strands of colorful silk threads would have been tied onto them. These bunches are called "Sprouts Qiao".

At dusk on Double Seventh Day, both teenager and unmarried grown-up girls of the villages will elect a pretty smart girl who is unanimously acknowledged as the most outstanding one as the leader. Under her command, a model of Queen Qiao will be handmade with tender willow twigs. A wooden scoop, which serves as the head, will be covered with painted paper to make the face. The body will be dressed up with beautiful clothes. Then it is placed under a willow shade or in the center of the courtyard. When darkness thickens, girls place incense burners, plates of fruits, steamed figurines made of flour and their embroidery works on the desk in front of Queen Qiao. They kneel down on the ground in reverence, holding one bowl in each hand and start singing Qiqiao songs ...

Their singing, to the rhythmic rubbing of the two bowls, is usually sweet and emotional, carried far away in the summer breeze of the night. The singing will last till three incenses have been burnt, then the Welcoming ceremony comes to an end.

When evening finally sinks in and the moon is high in the sky, the time for the most important part of the ritual

Chapter III
A Study on the Folk Story, the Cow Culture and the Qiqiao Customs
Popular in Eastern Gansu and Shaanxi Provinces
077

involving fortune-telling and appraisal of needleworks finally comes. Girls put a basin of clean water in front of the model of Queen Qiao, pinch a part of their bean sprout bundle off, and throw it into the water. It is believed that the messages from Queen Qiao about one's future and marriage, whether she will be blessed with superior needlework skills or not, are all hidden in the shadows of bean sprouts cast on the bottom of the water basin by the moonlight. If it looks like a spinning wheel, a loom, or a flower, it means that the girl is a good hand in weaving, embroidering, and all kinds of needlework. If the shadow looks like a cutting knife, a ladle, or pots and bowls, it means that the girl will be a good cook. If the shadow looks like a phoenix coronet and robes of rank, it means that the girl will marry well into a wealthy or influential family... This part is called "pinching the sprouts Qiao". When this is done, two girls will hold their hands together to make a sedan for Queen Qiao, on which the latter will be seated and escorted by all the girls in lines to the nearest pond or riverbank where a seeing-off ceremony will take place before the goddess embarks on her way back to meet her husband, the Cowherd, in the sky.

Some girls even stay up late in a hope of witnessing the reunion of the couple. They stoop over the edge of a well, holding their breath to look at the well water, as they are told by the eldest in the village that if they are quiet enough, they can see the reflections of the couple from the sky. Some others eavesdrop under the grapevines for affectionate murmuring of the couple, wishing to share their happiness ...

As Double Seventh Day (or the Qixi Festival) falls at a time when a new harvest of grain has just been made, it's a tradition for every family to mill flour with newly harvested wheat for wheaten-food making. Girls will steam or fry figurines of human beings, animals and plants, which are called "figurines Qiao", to give as gifts to the kids of the extended family. This is called "Qiao-sharing"[1].

In the book *The Folk Customs of Eastern Gansu Province*, there is a paragraph about the festive celebrations on Double Seventh Day in that area:

Qiqiao is a festival for girls. Early in the morning, girls go into the high grasses in the wild to "get moistened by the morning dew". They then put various kinds of grain seeds, usually 7 pieces of each, into a china basin of clean water for germination. The growing speed of the seeds will be an important indicator of whether the girl is smart or not, or whether she will be blessed with a Mr. Right and nice in-laws who will grant her a happy life in the future. Some girls even start to germinate bean sprouts in a water urn as early as on June 6th. On the evening of the Double Seventh, seven or eight girls get together, putting their bean sprouts into a water basin one by one to see what fate has in store for them. Meanwhile, the lovers go cuddle together under grapevines for eavesdropping on the couple in the sky. On this day, magpies are nowhere to be seen because, according to the elders of the village, they are away on a duty to make a bridge over the Milky Way with their body for the reunion of the star-crossed couple. That's why all

---

[1] Qiao-sharing means to share good luck, happiness and all the blessings from Queen Qiao. It is a ritual to show one's good will towards others.

Chapter III
A Study on the Folk Story, the Cow Culture and the Qiqiao Customs
Popular in Eastern Gansu and Shaanxi Provinces | 079

七夕文化透视 ▸▸▸
The Cowherd and the Weaver Fairy
A Study on the Folk Story and Double Seventh Day

the magpies you ever lay your eyes on afterward are bald, as their head feather would have been trodden on too much and worn thin on that day.

From this we can see that the Qiqiao customs in eastern Gansu have much in common with those in Xihe and eastern Lixian county, including towns like Yongxing and Yanguan, in the following aspects:

I. All the participants are teenage or unmarried grown-up girls only;

II. Bean sprouts are a necessity in fortune-telling, which is based on the interpretation of the shape of shadows;

III. A model of Queen Qiao is a must for girls to worship, offer incense and sacrifices;

IV. In both cases, age-old Qiqiao songs are sung in front of the model of Queen Qiao;

V. Certain procedures are followed in the process of sacrificial rites;

VI. In both cases, it is a tradition to eavesdrop on the couple under grapevines on the evening of Double Seventh;

VII. There is a tradition of seeing Queen Qiao off by burning a model by the riverside at midnight on the Double Seventh.

But there are differences, too:

I. In the north and the middle areas of Xihe as well as in Yongxing and Yanguan in Lixian county, Qiqiao celebrations

last for 7 days and 8 nights, which is much longer than in the eastern Gansu area;

II. The celebrations in Xihe and Lixian include not only singing, but also dancing. Girls hold hands dancing and singing, but not accompanied by rubbing bowls;

III. The girls in Xihe and Lixian counties exchange visits between the celebrating groups of nearby neighborhoods for learning, performing, communicating and socializing. It is not the case in eastern Gansu.

IV. In Xihe county, there is no tradition of giving flour figurines as gifts to the kids in the family and friends.

V. In Xihe and Lixian counties, girls do not go to the wilderness to "get moistened by the morning dew";

VI. In Xihe and Lixian counties, there is not a tradition of looking into the well water for the reflections of the Weaver Fairy and the Cowherd.

In comparison, Qiqiao celebrations in eastern Gansu last much shorter, and the worship rituals are simpler. The traditions of giving off flour pastries made of newly harvested wheat, or the girls' getting moistened by the morning dew, etc. show more influences and cultural relics of a farming society.

Many counties in Shaanxi province keep traditions similar to those in eastern Gansu, but the relevant historical records are so concise that they can be confusing when the narrations are mixed up. An example comes from "The Folk Customs" in volume 1 of *The County Annals of Xianyang* (《咸阳县志》) compiled during the reign of Emperor Qianlong: "On the 7th day of July, girls celebrate

Chapter III
A Study on the Folk Story, the Cow Culture and the Qiqiao Customs | 081
Popular in Eastern Gansu and Shaanxi Provinces

七夕文化透视 ▶▶▶
The Cowherd and the Weaver Fairy
A Study on the Folk Story and Double Seventh Day

the Qiqiao Festival with the offering of bean sprouts as a sacrifice while worshiping and praying." The record is so sketchy that the procedure is not clearly explained. Of course it's possible that the intellectuals (men only in feudal China) knew little about the girls' festival. Another example comes from *The County Annals of Xingping* (《兴平县志》):

> On Double Seventh Day, unmarried girls will germinate bean sprouts in clean water, which is called "Queen Qiao".

This account is quite misleading, as it tries to convince readers that girls start germinating bean sprouts on the very day. But it's impossible to have them ready for celebration or "Qiqiao" activity in one day. Besides, the bean sprouts is mistakenly tagged with the name "Queen Qiao". What a ridiculous mistake! Still, another example is from "The Local Customs" in *The County Annals of Gaoling* (《高陵县志·县俗》):

> On the 7th of lunar July, girls germinate grain seeds to pray for good luck and good needlework skills. Their deftness and intelligence are appraised through the skills they show in pulling thin silk thread fast through needle eyes by the lamplight.

Here the same mistake is repeated: wrong time and wrong procedure. In "The Local Customs" in volume 9 of *The County Annals of Fuping*, we read sentences like this: "On the 7th of lunar July, under the moonlight, fruits and melons are served on the desk placed in the courtyard. It is called Qiqiao." Fuping is located north

to Gaoling county. In "The Yearly Celebrations and Customs" (《民俗岁事》) in volume 6 of *The County Annals of Dali* (《大荔县志》), there is an account:

> On the evening of Double Seventh Day, unmarried girls put fruits, melons, drinks, delicacies and bean sprouts of around a foot long which they have germinated beforehand, on the desk. They then place it in the courtyard for the worship of Queen Qiao. They try to show their deftness in pulling thin silk thread through the tiny needle eyes to pray for good luck and superior needlework skills from Queen Qiao.

Dali county is located in the east of Middle Shaanxi province. "The Local Customs" in volume 4 of *The County Annals of Yongshou* recorded the event like this:

> On Double Seventh Day, young girls and kids set fruits, melons and bean sprouts on desks to worship the Weaver Fairy.

Wang Tinggui recorded in volume 6 of *The County Annals of Xingping* which he recompiled during the years of the Republic of China:

> Qiqiao: On Double Seventh Day, girls pray on their knees for blessings on their marriage and future as well as outstanding skills in needlework. This is the day on which the Weaver Fairy and her husband the Cowherd are believed to reunite.

All those accounts fail to give a clear description of the

Chapter III
A Study on the Folk Story, the Cow Culture and the Qiqiao Customs | 083
Popular in Eastern Gansu and Shaanxi Provinces

七夕文化透视 ▶▶▶
The Cowherd and the Weaver Fairy
A Study on the Folk Story and Double Seventh Day

procedures and local features of Qiqiao celebrations. The account in the hand-copied version of "The Local Customs and Yearly Celebrations" from volume 4 of *The County Annals of Tongguan* (《同关县志》) goes like the following:

> On Double Seventh Day, there is a folk custom of steaming chicken and wheaten food to give as gifts. Young girls offer sacrifices of fruits, wine and bean sprouts on desks before they kneel down to worship the Weaver Fairy (Queen Qiao). Then, the bean sprouts are cast into a bowl of clean water. The shadows cast on the bottom of the bowl by the moonlight are believed to carry hidden messages from Queen Qiao regarding the girl's fate or her appraisal of the girl's needlework skill (whether she is blessed, skilled or not). Besides, girls compete to thread seven needle eyes in the shortest time under the moonlight, or make wax baby figurines to float in water, which is believed to bring you good luck in giving offspring—the top priority for a married woman in feudal China.

Tongguan county in the Qing Dynasty is now where Tongchuan city is located, to the east of Xunyi county. The custom of floating wax baby figurines in water has not been heard of in other places. This is a proof of the colorfulness and diversification of Qiqiao customs in this area, which had been neglected by pedantic compilers who shut themselves down in their study and turned a blind eye to what was going on in the fields. In "The Folk Customs" of volume 2 of *The Sequence to the County Annals of Weinan* (《新续渭南县志》), there is another account:

On the evening of Double Seventh, girls offer sacrifices of fruits and melons to worship the Weaver Fairy. They float needles in water to test whether a girl is deft or not. It is called "Qiqiao". This is exactly what was recorded in *A Miscellaneous Work from Chang'an* about the court ladies threading 7 needle eyes on Kaijin Pavilion.

The County Annals of Fengxian (《凤县志》) recorded the event like this:

On the 7th of lunar July, a common practice among local private schools is for the pupils to compete in improvising poems and essays in seminars which are copiously provided with drinks and delicacies. In the evening, girls convene for Qiqiao celebrations with fruits and melons lavishly offered on the desks in the courtyard. According to the local custom, girls will germinate bean sprouts in clean water since June, which will grow to something about 2 feet long by Double Seventh. If the sprouts are too short, the grower will fell so ashamed that they refuse to offer them to Queen Qiao. The shadows cast on the bottom of the water basin will be decoded as a sign of the girl's deftness in needlework, or as an omen on her future.

This is a more detailed recording of what really happens on the evening of the Double Seventh. The relevant descriptions in "The Folk Customs" from volume 12 of *The Sequence to the County Annals of Liquan* (《续修礼泉县志稿》) goes like this:

Chapter III
A Study on the Folk Story, the Cow Culture and the Qiqiao Customs
Popular in Eastern Gansu and Shaanxi Provinces | 085

The Qiqiao Festival falls on the 7th of lunar July. On the evening, fruits and melons are offered, and incense is burned. Young girls and kids will make shoes and socks with colorful papers as a sacrifice to Queen Qiao.

From the custom of making colorful paper shoes and socks, we can notice a similarity with the custom of making models of Queen Qiao with bamboo and wood before dressing then up in colorful clothes for worship in eastern Gansu, as recorded in *The Folk Customs of Zhengning*. It is possible that the custom was reduced to a simple, symbolic ritual when it was spread out and passed down.

From all the information above, we can see that eastern Gansu and the central area of Shaanxi province share a tradition of Qiqiao celebrations which are quite similar in general, with only minor differences among different regions. Of course, it's possible that the regional differences are only the result of a too sketchy accounts which failed to give a comprehensive and precise picture of the event. In the north and south there are similar customs about which we will not go into details here.

Judging from the Qiqiao songs circulated in eastern Gansu, the Double Seventh celebrations used to be loaded with cultural connotations. A sentence from "A Collective Records of the Folk Customs" (《风俗志》) from volume 13 of *The County Annals of Zhenyuan* reads:

> On the day, girls will prepare fruits, delicacies, tea and wine as snacks so that they can get together to stay up late embroidering and praying for blessings from Queen Qiao in the evening.

Getting together to embroider is on one hand an effort to

communicate so as to improve their needlework skills on the very festival dedicated to Queen Qiao, but on the other hand to celebrate the reunion of the couple.

Something that deserves our special attention is that singing in celebrations is a shared tradition in eastern Gansu, Xihe and the South of Lixian county. Just like in the latter two areas, the songs circulated in eastern Gansu include both traditional ones and new compositions. Let's take two pieces from Zhengning county as examples of traditional ones:

> Come my friends on this day,
> to welcome the lady of Milky Way.
> Once the Southern Gate is wide open,
> of her descending it is a token.

> Through the Gate and by the cloud,
> "Queen Qiao's coming!" I shout aloud.
> Come along is the protector of farmer,
> Cowherd is a blessing to my father.

> I will feed the old golden cow,
> so I can expect a good harvest in store.
> Farming hard and reading a lot,
> I will be blessed with a never-empty pot.

> To dear Lady Qiao I offer a sweet pear,
> a plum blossom is cut out as I stare;
> To dear Lady Qiao I offer a juicy melon,

Chapter III
A Study on the Folk Story, the Cow Culture and the Qiqiao Customs
Popular in Eastern Gansu and Shaanxi Provinces | 087

a chrysanthemum is vivid in my draft pattern.

To dear Lady Qiao I offer a bowl of honey,
love birds I cut no longer look funny;
To dear Lady Qiao I offer a big peach,
and I'm tutored in every embroidery stitch.

To dear Lady Qiao I offer red dates,
padded jacket is now done with much ease;
To dear Lady Qiao I offer pearly grapes,
about quilt-sewing she gives me tips.

To dear Lady Qiao I offer a freshly-picked apple,
the trick of bun-making I easily handle[1];
My lady Qiao so dear and nice,
teach me all the skills she tries.

Paper cutting is a popular entertainment and necessary skill for women in eastern Gansu to command. The windows plastered with white paper are decorated with red paper cuttings of different patterns, including plants, animals and characters which feature fairy tales and legends. Girls compete in the originality and complexity of the patterns they cut. The Qiqiao song quoted above is mostly about paper cutting skills that girls want to acquire, which is similar in theme to the one titled "Queen Qiao" from the Tianshui area.

---

[1] In reference to *The Folk Customs of Zhengning* by Wang Changsheng. Steaming buns are staple food in northern China, so bun-making is regarded a necessary expertise that is expected from a qualified housewife.

The following is another song "Queen Qiao" which is popular in Huating county of Pingliang:

Once a year there is a 7th of July,
which allows a reunion in the sky.
Come down to us, dear Lady Qiao,
we need you here quite as well.

Bless young lads with ink and brush.
Bless young girls with needle and threads.
With ink and brush a lot lads will achieve,
with needle and threads a lot girls will weave.

Reading and writing, sewing and weaving,
We will be blessed with a good living.

From the Qiqiao songs circulated in eastern Gansu, we can see that the Qiqiao celebrations were once conducted ceremoniously in this area. Judging from the story of "The Cowherd and the Weaver Fairy" recorded on Yunmeng Bamboo slips from the Qin Dynasty which was unearthed in Hubei province, and also from the construction of a bridge over the Wei River imitating the one over the Milky Way as was recorded in *Sanfu Huangtu*, Double Seventh Day in the Qin Dynasty was still a day dedicated to honoring the star-crossed couple and celebrating their reunion. Furthermore, taking the two poems "A Woodcutter's Love" and "The Reed" into consideration, the festival in Ancient Times was only an occasion on which young men and women expressed their longing for sweet love and freedom in marriage, so was tainted with a tragic color.

Chapter III
A Study on the Folk Story, the Cow Culture and the Qiqiao Customs
Popular in Eastern Gansu and Shaanxi Provinces

089

七夕文化透视 ▶▶▶
The Cowherd and the Weaver Fairy
A Study on the Folk Story and Double Seventh Day

However, according to what was recorded in *A Miscellaneous Work from Chang'an*, by the time of the Han royal court, the day had already been celebrated as a festival of colorful entertainments. On the day, young court ladies who had left their families at a young age to live in isolated palace quarters among other girls from all over the country gathered to entertain themselves in the old way as they were still at home. It was not only a way to alleviate their homesickness and a retrospection on their carefree maiden years, but also a valuable occasion for socialization and relaxation. The strict court rituals and disciplines, of course, did not allow the celebration of the festival as one which honored free love and marriage between young men and women, as was practiced in folk traditions, as the emperor was supposed to be the only "man" for all of them. Having been separated from their families and the ordinary life of love and marriage, although affluently provided in material, young women then turned the festival into a day for entertaining competitions such as showcasing their needlework skills and craftsmanship. Noble families soon followed suit as the royal court was always the bench-making power in various aspects of social life in feudal China. Intellectuals who were part of the noble class wrote down the festive customs familiar to them, thus helped promote those activities in the whole society. The stone statues of the Cowherd and the Weaver Fairy erected by Kunming lake in the Western Han Dynasty is a solid proof of the popularization of the folk story and the festival.

Another possible reason for the popularity of the folk story as well as Double Seventh Day during the Western and Eastern Han Dynasties is, according to *The Story about Emperor Wu of the Han Dynasty* (《汉武故事》), that Emperor Wu of the Western Han Dynasty was born on lunar July 7th. Besides, according to "A Biography of Emperor Wu" in *The*

Book of the Han Dynasty (《汉书·武帝纪》), the emperor was officially designated as the crown prince when he was seven years old. An anecdote recorded in *The Story about the Emperor Wudi of Han* goes like this:

> A courier from the Queen Mother of the West told the emperor: "I will come for a short visit on seventh of July." The emperor went to the Chenghua Palace on the day and lit up radiant lampads.

Then,

> On the seventh of lunar July, Emperor Wu, who was observing fast in Chenghua Palace, saw a flock of green birds[1] descending into the courtyard. When he consulted his wise minister Dongfang Shuo about this, he was told: "The Queen Mother of the West intends to honor us with her presence at dusk. We'd better do cleaning to welcome her majesty."[2]

The two volumes of *The Story about Emperor Wu of the Han Dynasty* were mentioned in *A Miscellaneous Work from Chang'an* by Ge Hong, but the author was not mentioned. However, in *Sanfu Huangtu*, it is attributed to Ban Gu, the author of *The Book of the Han Dynasty*. According to the latest research, the book was most probably finished during the Han and Wei Dynasties but underwent amendments later. In *The Story about Emperor Wu of the Han*

[1]　In Chinese fairy tales, green bird serves as the courier and dinner attendant to the Mother Queen of the West.

[2]　For *The Story about the Emperor Wu of the Han Dynasty,* please refer to Volume 1 of *The Series of Compilation of Ancient Works by Luxun* (《鲁迅辑录古籍丛编》), published by the Publishing House of People's Literature in 1999, pp. 424-425.

Chapter III
A Study on the Folk Story, the Cow Culture and the Qiqiao Customs
Popular in Eastern Gansu and Shaanxi Provinces　091

七夕文化透视 ▶▶▶
The Cowherd and the Weaver Fairy
A Study on the Folk Story and Double Seventh Day

Dynasty from volume 52 of the handwritten copy of *Shuofu* from the Ming Dynasty, the following lines are found: "A lady Xu with a pseudonym Yijun from Changling prefecture was good at sorcery. Though already 137 years old during the middle of Yuanyan years under the reign of present Emperor Chengdi, she looked like a young girl." Li Jianguo took it as a proof of the book's completion under the reign of Emperor Cheng[①] of the Han Dynasty. From the above story, we can see that Double Seventh Day had already become an important festival during the Western Han Dynasty, tinted with the color of the folk story "The Cowherd and the Weaver Fairy" already.

Originally a story venting out the working class' hatred toward feudal ethics and ruling system of influential families, and at the same time expressing their longing for marital freedom, the story "The Cowherd and the Weaver Fairy" was involved in festive activities such as praying or competitions. This was actually a compromise between folk practice and the increasingly consolidated feudal ethics which intentionally highlighted the Weaver Fairy's deftness in terms of needlework but effaced her existence as a defiant fighter for personal happiness so as to make her an idol for young girls to worship in gender education. That explains the later popularization of Qiqiao activities in the whole society later.

Besides, numerous poems by poets from eastern Gansu and central Shaanxi either depict Double Seventh Day or refer to it in their poems through which the grandeur of the festive celebrations in ancient times can still be felt.

There are also other artistic creations related to the Festival and

---

[①] Reference to *A History of Pre-Tang Supernatural Stories* (《唐前志怪小说史》) writtern by Li Jianguo and published by Tianjin Educational Publishing House in 2005, p. 181.

the couple, such as a local drama titled exactly "The Weaver Fairy and the Cowherd" as well as a puppet shadow show called "The Reunion on Double Seventh Day" (《七夕会》) in eastern Gansu.

Last but not least, I must mention the temple dedicated to the Queen Mother of the West on Hui Mountain located at the intersection of the Jing River and the Rui River to the west of the Jingchuan county of Pingliang city, Gansu province. A grotto architecture inside and a wooden structure outside, the temple, which was built during the Yuanfeng years of the Western Han Dynasty, hosts a statue of the Queen Mother of the West. It has been regarded as the oldest temple dedicated to the fairy Queen mother. Four times a year the temple fair is held: the first on lunar March 20th, the second on the Double Fifth Festival, the third on the so-called birthday of the Queen Mother, lunar July 18th, and the last in lunar September. Among the four, the first one on March 20th is the grandest in scale, as it marks the day when the temple was rebuilt during the first year of the Kaibao period of the Song Dynasty (to be exact, in the year 968 A.D.). On this day, believers from Jingchuan, Chongxin, Huating, Lingtai, Zhenyuan, Pingliang, Xifeng of Gansu province, as well as from counties like Changwu in Shaanxi province or even from other provinces, would come to worship, rain or shine. It was believed that Yaochi, the fairy pond, was located on the southern face of Mountain Hui. On lunar March 20th, people would flock to the mountain to offer incense, collect fairy spring water and watch performances. From this we can see the popularity of the fairy among the locals. Most probably, the Queen Mother of the West worshiped here is exactly the one mentioned in the folk story of "The Cowherd and the Weaver Fairy".

In conclusion, the early naming of "the Cowherd star" must

Chapter III
A Study on the Folk Story, the Cow Culture and the Qiqiao Customs
Popular in Eastern Gansu and Shaanxi Provinces

093

七夕文化透视 ▶▶▶
The Cowherd and the Weaver Fairy
A Study on the Folk Story and Double Seventh Day

have something to do with the ancestor of the Zhou people. Numerous stone statues, engravings, ancestral temples dedicated to the couple and other cultural relics discovered in the early habitat of the Zhou people in central Shaanxi and that of the Qin people in eastern Gansu, as well as the folk customs of cow worship and those related to tillage culture, indicate a strong bond between the local people and the two fairy figures. People's affection and trust in their animal working pals are clearly manifested in the folk story in which the Cowherd goes through all the tough times in his life with support and assistance of the ox. The cultural background provided a perfect hotbed which nurtured the image of the Cowherd, the touching story of mutual dependence between an ox and a man, and the relevant plots in "The Cowherd and the Weaver Fairy". An extensive study on those images, plots and customs will reveal much about the history of early agricultural development in our country and the rich connotations of cow-related culture in those areas.

Chapter IV
The Southward Spread of Qiqiao Customs

Section 1　The Migration of the Hakka People and the Southward Spread of the Qiqiao Festival

With the rise of Confucianism as the main state ideology in the Han Dynasty, the folk customs concerning Double Seventh Day started to focus further on Qiqiao, i.e. to pray for blessings, especially in marriage and needlework expertise from Queen Qiao, or in other words, the Weaver Fairy. During the Han Dynasty, when the capital was relocated to Luoyang in the east, Double Seventh Day and the relevant folk customs were first brought to the Central Plains.

A dozen of years' upheavals between the shift of Western and Eastern Han Dynasties as well as that resumed at the end of the Eastern Han Dynasty led to large-scale migration. After the collapse of the Western Jin Dynasty, northern China fell into disunification and chaos of warfare. Warlords from the five Hu minorities including Xiongnu, Xianbei, Jie, Di and Qiang established their own dynasties, only to meet their destruction one by one. Northern China entered an era called "the Sixteen States" during which the wealthy and influential families migrated to the south, taking along with them historical documents and folk customs including those associated with Double Seventh Day. That initiated the rapid spread of the

七夕文化透视 ▶▶▶
The Cowherd and the Weaver Fairy
A Study on the Folk Story and Double Seventh Day

festival along with its ways of celebrations in the south. Afterwards, continuous warfare and more upheavals such as the Huangchao Uprising (875-884) in the north compelled more people to migrate to the south or southeast, furthered the dissemination of the folk story and the festival along the way. During the process, differences in natural environment and lifestyle resulted in adaptations and variations in the content, aesthetic flavor and the details of festive rituals.

The Hakka people played a key role in the spread of Double Seventh Day in Jiangnan and Lingnan areas. This is a question which should be given special attention but has been neglected in previous research. The festive customs popular in Jiangnan and Lingnan areas differ in many ways from those observed in the north, quite as the case with the central plots in the folk story "The Cowherd and the Weaver Fairy". Apart from a shift in time and space, I think it should be attributed mainly to the big difference in social status among the celebrants.

The term "Hakka", which means "guest" or "migrants", is the opposite of "aborigine", which signifies "original inhabitants or natives". The ancestors of Hakka were officials and the rich in the north. Because of warfare and shift of dynasties, they migrated to the south in large scale under the protection of armed escorts. For safety, they chose to live together in square or round fort dorks with spacious courtyard, which formed a relatively independent living space and protected them well from the looting of aborigines. In contrast to the individual immigrants who had to give up their usual ways and customs for better adaptation to the local life, Hakkas, in this way, were able to keep their way of northern life. Because of the language, customs and habits which were obviously different from

those of the local, the latter called them Hakkas, meaning "the late-comers who are not aborigines". For example, in some areas, Hakkas keep the custom of "digging wells on lunar July 7th" till today. In Fuchen county, Fujian province, it is mentioned that "People eat peach kernels and dig wells on July 7th." ("The Festive Customs" from *An Extensive Collection of Literature of All Times*,《古今图书集成·岁功典》) A similar custom is observed in Gong'an county of Hubei province. "Well-digging" is obviously a custom brought from the north which was closely related to agricultural cultivation.

In Guangdong province, the eastern counties are home to the largest and most prosperous Hakka communities. These eastern counties include Guangzhou and Dongguan and other surbodinate counties such as Lianping, Hepiing, Longchuan, Zijin of Heyuan city, Longmen and Boluo, as well as Huiyang district of Huizhou city, Xinfeng county of Shaoguan city and Baoan district of Shenzhen city. Even today, the Hakka people still keep the virtues of diligence and perseverance that have been handed down from their ancestors during the tough times of migration and resettlement.

The immigration history of the Hakka people in Guangdong province was recorded in numerous documents. Referring to the results of academic research, we can divide it roughly into five phases:

Phase 1: Since the end of the Western Jin Dynasty, continuous warfare caused by minority Hu groups dragged the whole northern society into chaos. Gentry families from the north moved southward from the Central Plains to the south of Hubei and He'nan province, or the area along the Yangzi River which belongs to Anhei and Jiangxi provinces, or along the Ganjiang River. You may find relevant records of the process in historical documents and genealogical charts. Tracing along the history of large-scale migration in China, we may find that it started even earlier, as early as in the Xia, Shang and Western Zhou Dynasties. Many tribes or nationalities migrated from the north to the south during that time. As for the large-scale organized southward immigration, it started from the unification of China as one centralized empire for the first time in history by Emperor Shihuang of the Qin Dynasty. He dispatched tens of thousands of soldiers into the depth of Lingnan area for border defence, and another 500 thousands to excavate Lingqu Canal in Lingnan. This resulted in a significant number of soldiers and migrants settling permanently in the area. During the Pre-Qin times, the folk story "The Cowherd and the Weaver Fairy" had not yet taken on its later shape, no had the Double Seventh Day and the relevant customs. Moreover, as the frontier soldiers had limited access to intact, normal family or social life, it was not likely that the festive celebrations (especially those celebrated exclusively by women) would raise their attention or arouse their interest. Those immigrations which were irrelevant to the spread of Double Seventh Day and its customs thus will be skipped here. As for the small-scale immigrations during the Western and Eastern Han Dynasties when people sought shelter from wars by moving to nearby secluded areas, we will still dismiss from our discussion. Since the system of influential and dominant families had not been fully established during that time, the well organized, long-distance, large-scale southward immigration like what happened much later in history did not happen then. The short-distance, small-scale immigration mentioned above exerted a very limited influence in relatively small sphere, which paled in comparison to those started from the end of the Western Jin Dynasty.

Phase 2: Affected by the Huangchao Uprising at the end of the

Tang Dynasty, Hakka families moved again from where they had settled down in Phase 1 in Anhui, Henan and Jiangxi, further to the south of Anhui, the southeast of Jiangxi, the southwest of Fujian and the northeastern border of Guangdong province. In volume 2 "Families" (《氏族》) in *Chongzheng Genealogical Chart of Hakka* (《崇正同人系谱》), under the entry of "Family Xue" it was recorded: "Some branches of family Xue moved southward to Ninghua and Shibi of Fujian province during the Huangchao Uprising at the end of the Tang Dynasty. During the Yuan Dynasty when Xuexin headed the clan, he moved the clan again from Ninghua to Pingyuan of Guangdong province." The entry for "Family Wu" reads:

> The family had lived in Bohai for generations, with only a few branches living apart in Zhongzhou. At the end of the Tang Dynasty, the family followed Wang Chao, a warlord, and moved to Fujian. They headed to Chaozhou and Jiaying before finally settled down there.

The entry for "Family Gu" goes as follows:

> The ancestor of the Gu's had lived in Hongzhou before he moved to Gufan during the Five Dynasties. He was born in the year 877 (during the Tang Dynasty) and assumed the position of a Military Staff Officer of Baozhou. In the upheavals of the Central Plains at the end of the Tang Dynasty, he was forced to move his family southward to Lingnan area. Among his six sons, the eldest, Quanjiao, settled down in Guyun, the second eldest, Quangui, in Jiangxia, the third, Quanze, in Baisha,

七夕文化透视 ▸▸▸
The Cowherd and the Weaver Fairy
A Study on the Folk Story and Double Seventh Day

the fourth, Quanwang, in Zengcheng, the fifth, Quanrang, in Huizhou, and the youngest, Quanshang, in Gaozhou.[①]

Another example is from "A Research on Local Celebrity Master Luo of the Song Dynasty" (《宋乡贤罗学士遗事考略》) quoted from *The Genealogical Chart of Family Luo of Xingguo Prefecture* (《兴国州罗氏家谱》):

> Chang Ru, whose family had been living in Yuzhang for generations, passed the highest imperial examination and became Jinshi (进士) under the reign of Emperor Zhaozong of the Tang Dynasty. He was then dispatched to Xunzhou as the inquisitor. During the Huangchao Uprising, the road back to his hometown was blocked, so he was forced to drift outside.

The jurisdiction of Xunzhou in the Tang Dynasty covered many counties and cities around or to the northwest of what is now Longchuan county, including Longchuan, Heping, Xingning, Wuhua and Lianping in Guangdong province. In *The genealogical Chart of Family He of Xingning* (《兴宁何氏族谱》), you may find an entry that reads like this:

> ... first-named as Dan, he was born into a family in Lujiang of Zhili, Nanjing, in the year 892 of the Tang Dynasty ... In the year 922, Zhu Youying assumed the position of county magistrate ... In the following year, when his tenure of office ended, he went to Meizhou, then headed to Chaozhou, and finally settled down in Yanqian ...

---

① Both the quotations are from the book *Chongzheng Genealogical Chart of Hakka* (volume 1) compiled by Lai Jixi and Hanlin, 1995.

This account supports the idea that numerous official or influential families moved to the east of Guangdong province during the Tang and Song Dynasties.

Phase 3: From the end of the Northern Song Dynasty to the end of the Southern Song Dynasty. After the southward move of the royal court to Hangzhou during the reign of Emperor Gaozong of the Song Dynasty, under the influence of continuous upheavals including the southward aggression of the Jin ethnicity and the establishment of the Yuan Dynasty in the Central Plains, the ancestors of the Hakka people were pushed further south from their previous habitat they had taken in Phase 2, that is, to the east and north of Guangdong province. According to *The Genealogical Chart of Family Wei in Wuhua* (《五华魏氏族谱》):

> Approaching the end of the Song Dynasty, everywhere was in chaos.... My ancestors were so worried that they convened to discuss the possibility of moving the family to a safer place.... Thus the four brothers were forced to split up at Ninghua and take different roads. Their respective settlement choices were: Brother Yuan in Changle of Huizhou (now Wuhua) as the earliest ancestor of this family here.... Brother Xiang with the courtesy name Guotong, in Shanghang of Tingzhou, Fujian province, then moved to Longchuan of Huizhou city.
>
> ...

In numerous other genealogical charts of Hakka families in Xingning, Heping, Meizhou, Shixing, Nanxiong and Jiaying, you may find very detailed accounts of the family's migration history to

七夕文化透视 ▶▶▶
The Cowherd and the Weaver Fairy
A Study on the Folk Story and Double Seventh Day

Guangdong province during or at the end of the Song Dynasty or at the beginning of the Yuan Dynasty. There are other families whose exact time of migration from Fujian to Guangdong is unknown, but a close study on their genealogical shifts leads to the same conclusion. Families falling into this category include Family Wu, Family He, Family Zhang, Family Wen, Family Wu, Family Luo, Family Huang, Family Liao, etc. Almost all these families originated in the Central Plains.

Phase 4: Since the end of the Ming Dynasty and the beginning of the Qing Dynasty. Influenced by the dominance of Man ethinicity in the Central Plains, some of the early Hakka pioneers moved once again from their previous habitat in Phase 2 and Phase 3 to the central area of Guangdong province and the other coastal areas.

Phase 5: Since the reign of Emperor Tongzhi of the Qing Dynasty, the large-scale armed conflicts between the Hakka people and the aborigines in western Guangdong, as well as the influence of the Taiping Heavenly Kingdom, forced some of Hakkas to move to the south of Guangdong and Island Hainan.

Till today, there are still many ancient constructions like ancestral temples of Hakka people in Dongguan city which were built exactly in the style popular in the Central Plains during the Ming and Qing Dynasties to honor their native place.

Because most Hakkas were from official, wealthy or influential families that migrated from the north, they attached great importance to the preservation of their old way of life and customs which were once followed by their ancestors. This is a manifestation of their collective memories and emotional bond with their ancestors as well as their native place. Hakka people played a key role in the popularity of traditional festivals such as Double Fifth Day (the Dragon Boat

Festival in its southern version), Double Seventh Day, and the Mid-Autumn Festival in Guangdong province.

During the first phase of Hakka's southward migration, Qiqiao customs emerged in the Central Plains. Therefore, it is highly probable that they were brought to the south very early, but became popular as a festival later during the increasing cultural exchange.

Due attention should be paid to the fact that Double Seventh Day customs observed by Hakka people represented the aristocratic features exclusive to families of high social status in ancient north, rather than those of the grassroots. Some of these customs were directly inherited from their ancestors who were once members of the upper class in the Central Plains, while others are borrowed from Jiangxi, Zhejiang and Fujian provinces, which varied already in some way from their original forms back in the Central Plains. The folk story told among Hakka people is tinted strongly of intellectual ideology and taste. This provides a perfect explanation to the regional variations and colorful nature of Double Seventh Day celebrations in Guangdong province.

The following are some historical records about the festive customs observed in Guangdong province. For example, the time of the festive celebration is in accordance with that observed by the Southern Tang royal court during the time of the Five Dynasties. In *The Prefecture Annals of Deqing* (《德庆州志》) compiled in the year 1899 (during the Qing Dynasty), we may find the following account:

> The Festival is mostly celebrated on the evening of lunar July 6th in Guangdong province. On the evening, girls offer wine, fruits and melons as sacrifices to the Weaver Fairy and the Cowherd to pay their respects.

七夕文化透视 ▸▸▸
The Cowherd and the Weaver Fairy
A Study on the Folk Story and Double Seventh Day

According to *The County Annals of Longshan* (《龙山县志》) compiled in 1930:

> On the evening of lunar July 6th[①], girls offer fruits and flowers as sacrifices to pray for blessings from the Weaver Fairy.

Longshan town, which was once Longshan county, is located to the north of Guangzhou and the east of Qingyuan city. Ni Hong wrote in his "A Zhuzhi Poem on Guangzhou" (《广州竹枝词》): "To pray for Mr. Right and a happy marriage, girls offer sacrifices on the day previous." Wang Zhaoquan of Panyu district in Guangzhou wrote in his "A Zhuzhi Poem on Yangcheng (now Guangzhou)" (《羊城竹枝词》): "On July 6th every girl in Lingnan worships Niulang (the Cowherd), and the fragrance from fruits and flowers drifts all around." In *An Encyclopedia of National Folk Customs* (《中华全国风俗志》) by Hu Pu'an, there is a paragraph introducing the festive customs related to the Double Seventh in Guangzhou:

> Double Seventh Day is celebrated ceremoniously in Guangzhou on the evening of lunar July 6th. A bridge is built in a spacious courtyard to mimic the magpie bridge over the Milky Way. Girls offer fruits and melons as sacrifices on tables, burn incense sticks, and light up big candles on desks. They then seat themselves in beautiful make-up in lines among embroidery screens. On the evening, people are welcome for visit, and

---

① The celebration on 6th is a practice which initiated from the end of the Tang Dynasty and the Five Dynasties. For reference, please see *Writings from Rongzhai Study*.

admission is not limited till the end of the magnificent event in the early hours of the following morning. The offerings on the desks include small household containers made of glutinous rice, or fake fruits and vegetables like longyan, lychee and lotus root made of flaxseeds. Exquisite and ingenious, all the handmade artifacts are a tribute of the maker's wisdom and deftness. A necessity for the occasion is a basin full of rice seedlings with roots covered with a thin layer of soil immersed in clear water. The green and lush seedlings are the result of intensive care in the increasingly hot weather.

All these accounts provide convincing proof of the tradition that Cantonese used to celebrate the Festival on the evening of July 6th .

But why? When and where did the custom originate? *An Extensive Collection of the Yearly Festivals and Customs* (《岁时广记》) by Chen Yuanliang of the Song Dynasty quoted from *Notes on Yearly Festival and Customs* (《岁时杂记》) which wrote: "Families in the capital celebrated the festival on the evening of lunar July 6th in the left wing of their house, but on lunar July 7th in the right wing." In Part III, volume 1 of *Writings from Rongzhai Study* (《容斋随笔·三笔》), the author wrote:

In lunar July of year 978, an imperial edict was issued: "The Double Seventh is such an important festival that its celebration had long been stipulated in court decree. But today many people celebrated it on July 6th instead of 7th, which is not in accordance with the tradition. From now on, the tradition of celebrationg it on the 7th should be restored." Anyway, titling it as the Double Seventh but celebrating it

七夕文化透视 ▶▶▶
The Cowherd and the Weaver Fairy
A Study on the Folk Story and Double Seventh Day

on the sixth is not a good practice by right and title. It is not known yet when the custom originated, but as there was no record of it during the Tang Dynasty, it is believed to have originated during the Five Dynasties.

Figure 14 Qiqiao Rites (2)

by Lu Haiyan

Lu You wrote in volume II of his *On the Years in Sichuan* (《入蜀记》):

On lunar July 5th, a military officer Wang Xuanlai talked about the festive customs related to Double Seventh Day. According to him, people in the Capital usually celebrated the festival on lunar July 6th, following the practice during the Southern Tang court when the princes, who were often stationed near the capital, celebrate the Festival with their wives and kids on the 6th. Early next morning, they would show up at the imperial feast to pay respects to their father, the king. This was then observed as a tradition.

Lu You was doubtful about this account, though it turned out to be partly the truth. In *A Casual Talk on Ways of the World during Wanli Years* (《万历野获编》) by Shen Defu of the Ming Dynasty, we find the following account:

The birthday of King Li Yu of the Southern Tang Dynasty falls on lunar July 7th. In order to celebrate it with him in Runzhou, his young brother usually celebrated the Qiqiao Festival with his own family in Yizhou on lunar July 6th. This practice became popular in Jiangsu and Zhejaing provinces later on. During the Chunhuan years of the Song Dynasty, an imperial edict set the celebration back on lunar July 7th. Therefore, the custom of its celebration on lunar July 6th started in the Southern Tang Dynasty.

七夕文化透视 ▸▸▸
The Cowherd and the Weaver Fairy
A Study on the Folk Story and Double Seventh Day

The record provided is concrete and reliable. According to what Wang Shizhen of the Qing Dynasty wrote in his *Notes of Xiangzu* (《香祖笔记》):

> It is not known yet when the custom of celebrating Double Seventh Day on the evening of July 6 originated ... According to *Records of Folk Customs in Kaifeng the East Capital,* "On the evenings of lunar July 6th and 7th, influential families would usually build a bamboo or wooden pavilion in their courtyard. It was gaily decorated and called the Qiqiao pavilion." From this, we can see that the festival was celebrated both on the 6th and 7th at that time. Later on, the tradition was unquestionably followed, but this practice has been abandoned now.

As a native of Qingxin city (now Huantai in Shandong province), Wang Shizhen's account only pertains to northern China, not including Guangdong province in the south. Deng Erya (1883-1954), a native of Dongguan city in modern history, described the grand celebrations of Double Seventh Day on lunar July 6th in his poem "A Zhuzhi Poem on July 7th of Year Guihai" (《癸亥年七夕竹枝词》, 1923). He added in the footnote :

> The custom of celebrating Double Seventh Day on the evening of lunar July 6th originated during the Five Dynasties when the ministers had to join the king in Qiqiao celebrations in the royal court on 7th.

That's why I believe that the Qiqiao customs among Hakka people in Guangdong are a heritage from the former upper class of

the north. They are mainly the descendants of ministers or aristocrats who were born and raised in the Central Plains. This explains why their celebration of the festival falls on the same day, i.e. on lunar July 6th, as that among the aristocrats of the north, but at a much later time.

Besides, either the rich display of offerings on desks or extensive participation of relatives and friends in Qiqiao rituals reflect the luxurious way of life typically associated with wealthy rather than the poor ones, for whom such practice would be unaffordable. We will go into more details on this discussion in the following section.

Section 2   Qiqiao Customs of the Hakka People and the Jubilee on Qijie's (the Seventh Sister's) Birthday

At the beginning of the Yuan Dynasty, with the spread of weaving skill which had been initiated by Huang Daopo to Jiangnan (the area to the south of the Yangtze River), weaving efficiency was greatly improved and the weaving business witnessed great development. Hakka people had brought the folk story about the Cowherd and the Weaver Fairy to the Lingnan area. Though tinged with an upper class flavor from the north, the festival still focused on the "Qiqiao" ritual in which the interpretation of the title "Weaver Fairy" is inevitable. From this perspective, the festival plays an important role in forstering women's creativity and enthusiasm towards weaving and needlework.

The original plot of the folk story revolves around a star-crossed couple who were separated from each other by force because of the great discrepancy in their social strata. Marriage or love between members from different social classes was taboo, both by the standard of feudal ideology and popular filial piety, let along the System of Dominant Family prevailing the Wei and Jin Dynasties. That explains why, under the rule of the Cao royal family of the Wei Dynasty, the story took on another form in which Dong Yong sold himself into slavery to obtain money for his father's burial. Moved by his filial piety toward his father, the Celestial Ruler (Jade Emperor) rewarded him by marrying a fairy (Weaver Fairy) to him to help out in his difficult situation. Once his debt was paid off, the Weaver Fairy left.

However, in the original story, the Cowherd and the Weaver Fairy married out of love and their own free will rather than under an order from a superior or a patriarch. Additionally, the Weaver Fairy was kidnapped to Heaven, and forced to leave her husband and kids instead of voluntarily abandoning them in a cold-hearted way once the "task" was done. (In the versions circulated in Jiangsu and Zhejiang provinces, the Weaver Fairy left at the first chance she was able to get hold of her dress that had been hidden by the Cowherd. When the Cowherd tried to catch up with her, she managed to stop him by drawing a line between them with a hairpin, which instantly turned into the Milky Way. In the northern version of the story, the Milky Way as a blockade to separate the couple was created by the Queen Mother of the West.) The story titled "Dong Yong" (《董永》) is actually an adaptation of "The Cowherd and the Weaver Fairy" to undermine the key plot in the latter that did not align with the ruling ideology of the Wei Dynasty.

The difference between the two stories is obvious: in the latter, the Weaver Fairy pursued freedom in love and marriage, but was separated by force from her family, while in the former, the Seventh Fairy Lady simply did her work as she was told to by her superior,

to act temporarily as Dong Yong's wife. In large-scale immigration from the north to the south in history, influential families naturally brought with them the story which perfectly fit their ethical standards, namely, "Dong Yong and the Seventh Fairy Lady". In this way, the Weaver Fairy was replaced by the Seventh Fairy Lady on the Qiqiao Festival. The heroine in the story "Dong Yong" (otherwise titled "An Encounter under a Locust Tree", or "Huaiyin Xianghui",《槐荫相会》) which is widely told in Jiangsu, Zhejiang and Guangdong provinces, is referred to as "the Seventh Fairy" just because the heroine in the story "The Cowherd and the Weaver Fairy" is believed to be the seventh daughter of the Jade Emperor.

In some areas of Guangdong province, Qiqiao celebrations are called "Jubilee on Qijie's (the Seventh Sister's) Birthday" (七姐诞), "the Seventh Sister Party" (七姐会), or "the worship of the Seventh Sister" (拜七姊). According to the section on customs in the third part of "Culture" in *The County Annals of Boluo County* (《博罗县志·文化三·风俗》):

> Young girls serve fruits and melons to pray for good needlework skill and good luck. They pool money to offer sacrifices to Queen Qiao and prepare delicacies as well as drinks for a get-together, which is called "the Seventh Sister Party" or "the worship of the Seventh Sister", as the Weaver Fairy is commonly known as the Seventh Sister among the locals.

This provides a solid proof of the connection between the two stories, which had escaped the notice of previous researchers for so many years.

Among the Hakka people in Guangdong province, there circulated another story apart from the one about the reunion of the

七夕文化透视 ▶▶▶
The Cowherd and the Weaver Fairy
A Study on the Folk Story and Double Seventh Day

Cowherd and the Weaver Fairy over the magpie bridge. It is said that Dong Zhongshu, the erudite scholar of the Han Dynasty, had a mother who was a fairy living in Heaven. She would descend to the mortal world once a year on the seventh of lunar July to bathe in a river. Dong Zhongshu managed a meeting with his mother by taking away her clothes left by the riverbank. This story seems to be a fusion of the story of Dong Yong and the story of "The Cowherd and the Weaver Fairy", as the couple in the former gave birth to a baby boy named Dong Zhong. This story coincides with the second part of the story titled "Tian Kunlun" (田昆仑) in *Anecdotes about Spirits and Immortals* (《搜神记》) by Gou Daoxing, which was uncovered in the Buddhist Scripture Cave of Dunhuang. The only difference is that the baby boy of the couple Tian Kunlun and the fairy is named Tianzhang, while the man who helped Tianzhang in his search for his mother is called Dongzhong. In reality, there was a famous sorcerer in history named Dongzhong. A quotation from *New Perspectives* (*Xinlun*, 《新论》) by Huan Tan of the Western Han Dynasty in volume 944 of *Imperial Readings of the Taiping Era* goes like this:

> Dong Zhong of Suiling is good at sorcery. Once put into prison on charges of a serious offence, he feigned illness and death. Several days after his death, when the body started to decay and worms began to wriggle out, it was discarded. Then Dong came back to life.

In the story "Dongyong Bianwen" which was unearthed in Dunhuang, Dong Zhong was mistakenly identified as the son of Dong Yong and the fairy. In Guangdong province, the mistake was further

propagated with the name Dong Zhongshu, the famous scholar. This error existed in the story-telling script "Dongyong's Encounter with a Fairy" (《董永遇仙记》) and the romance "The Romance of Brocade" (*Zhijing Ji*,《织锦记》) by Gu Jueyu of the Ming Dynasty.

As discussed earlier, the large-scale immigration of influential and wealthy families from the north to the south, which began at the end of the Western Jin Dynasty, brought Qiqiao customs and ways of celebrations to the south, which were later observed ceremoniously among Hakka people. Numerous poems and essays were written to honor the festival.

According to *A Collective Record of Nationwide Folk Customs* by Hu Pu'an which was quoted in the previous section, there are some richer and more detailed descriptions regarding Qiqiao celebrations:

The 7th of lunar July is the day when the Cowherd and the Weaver Fairy reunite. Usually, unmarried girls get together on this day for a Qiqiao party. In preparation, they would collect novel knickknacks and gadgets, making all kinds of artifacts such as fruits, figurine ladies, objects and even mansions with dry stem pith of rice-paper plants, colored paper, sesame, or rice grains for display or to compete with each other.

On the eve of the 7th (that is, on the evening of lunar July 6th), all these exquisite offerings are displayed on a desk laid out in the courtyard, along with needles, antiques, treasures, flowers, fruits and fragrant powder. There is such a myriad of beautiful objects that, in some cases, dozens of desks are laid out for a full display. Friends and relatives are invited, and blind female musicians are summoned for overnight musical accompaniment. Even poor families would manage a festive celebration for their daughters within their limited means so as to observe the tradition. Around eight o'clock in the evening, girls burn fragrant incense before kneeling down to pray for the descent of the fairy. From midnight to about five o'clock in the morning, they would pray seven times to accord with the title of the Weaver Fairy as the seventh sister. This is called "the worship of the fairy" (拜仙).

When this is done, they would try to thread needle eyes in dim light to prove their dexterity. If someone's thread goes smoothly through the needle eyes, she is believed to be deft and blessed by Queen Qiao, also known as "the Weaver Fairy". Then a round paper dressing basin is burned, with dresses, headscarves, powder boxes and combs all made of paper in seven copies. It is called the "dressing basin" (梳妆盆).

On the seventh day, all the objects are still on display, because all the rituals conducted on the previous night will be repeated, though under a different title of "worshiping the Cowherd", which would be headed by young boys. When the whole ritual is done, all the food and gadgets would be sent out as gifts to relatives and friends. Married women are not allowed in such celebrations, although newly married women in the first or second year of their marriage would conduct a ritual called the "adieu to the fairy" (辞仙礼).

They would offer meat, red eggs and sour gingers as sacrifices to the fairy so that they could be blessed with male offsprings. Pears, which symbolize "departure" or "separation" in Chinese culture are also offered, to bid farewell to the fairy. These are exclusive offerings only allowed for them. On the seventh day at noon, families with

young kids would worship under the eaves. After the ritual is done, a small paper dressing basin is burnt in the hope that the fairy will see to it that their kids are exempted from scabies. It is commonly believed that the god posted under the eaves is in charge of scabies and carbuncles giving.

On the following morning, people fetch clean water and store it in a sealed urn to make so-called "the double seventh water". This water can stay good and clear for a long time and is believed to work perfectly well on scabies.

There is a detailed description of the making of handmade artifacts as well as the procedures of "Worship the fairy". The customs of needle-threading and displaying fruits had been observed as early as in the Han Dynasty and have been kept in festive celebrations in many areas since.

Several other aspects of Qiqiao customs practiced in Guangdong province deserve our attention:

First, there is a rich display of abundant delicate gadgets and artifacts made of different materials, along with needles, fragrant powder, antiques, treasures, flowers and fruits for public appreciation and peer competition. In some cases, dozens of desks are used for the display, making it the most striking feature having no match in other places.

Second, in most parts of northern China, Qiqiao is a festival exclusively celebrated by women, mostly only unmarried girls. However, in Guangdong, young boys play a leading role in the sacrificial rites of "Cowherd-worshiping". In some Hakka habitat, people believe that Double Seventh Day is also the birthday of the God of Wisdom (文曲星), so intellectuals get together to offer sacrifices to the God, apart from celebrations involving feasting and drinking. That is called "the party

七夕文化透视 ▶▶▶
The Cowherd and the Weaver Fairy
A Study on the Folk Story and Double Seventh Day

dedicated to the God of Wisdom" (魁星会). Those two characteristics about Guangdong Qiqiao celebrations are tinted strikingly with the style and flavor of upper-class families in the north in early times.

Third, the ritual of worshiping gods and fairies has been lost in most areas of northern China, but is still observed in Xihe and the south of Lixian county. These areas including towns like Yongxing, Yanguan and Qishan, are located in the south of Gansu province. Compared with the Guangdong ritual involving paper dressing basin filled with dresses, headscarves, powder boxes and so on, the paper model of Queen Qiao (the Weaver Fairy) worshiped in Xihe and Lixian is more concrete and vivid. Though varied in forms, both customs must have derived from the same earlier ritual form observed in the north. Besides, in some areas of Guangdong such as Yingde, Xingning, Chixi and some Hakka habitats, there are customs of airing books and clothes under the sun on Double Seventh Day, which can be attributed to the damp-hot climate. This is also an age-old custom recorded in county annals as well as in a much earlier source *A Handbook and Calendar for Farming* by Cui Shi of the Eastern Han Dynasty. From all these examples we can see that the Double Seventh Day customs in Guangdong province have a long history. The main contents and forms of these customs must have come into being very early, reflecting their upper-class origin in the Central Plains.

When a folk custom is brought from one place to another, it inevitably undergoes certain adaptations or enrichment, in other words, localization. Some other particular features noticeable in the Double Seventh Day customs kept by Hakka people in Guangdong province include:

First, fetch Double Seventh Day water. The custom was recorded in volume 4 in *New Notes about Guangdong* (*Guangdong Xinyu*, 《广东新语》) by Qu Dajun, under the item titled "The Book

of Water". You can also read about it in other sources such as *The County Annals of Yingde*, *The Prefecture Annals of Huizhou*, *The County Annals of Boluo* and *The County Annals of Chixi*, etc.

Second, worship of a minor star beside Vega. According to "Customs" in *The County Annals of Yingde* (《英德县志·舆地下·风俗》):

> Beside Vega, there is a minor star. On the seventh of lunar July, women and girls stay up late into the night when it is quiet and peaceful. They burn fragrant incense and offer sacrifices to pray to the star for good look and fair countenance.

This custom is practiced in some parts of the Central Plains, too. For example, a quotation from *Beauty Tips of Huainan* (《淮南方华术》) in volume 3 of *Imperial Readings of the Taiping Era* reads like this:

> At noon on the seventh of lunar July, pick 7 leaves from a melon vine. Stand facing south in a northern room. Rub your face with the leaves tenderly, nevus and moles will disappear immediately.

Another quotation from *Monthly Records by Madame Wei* (《韦氏月录》) in the same volume goes like this:

> On the seventh of lunar July, mix the blood of a black-bone chicken with the powder of peach blossom picked on the third of March. Then smear the mixture over your face and body, and you will be rewarded with a countenance as fair and delicate as a piece of jade.

From this we can see that the Guangdong custom of girls praying for beauty on Double Seventh Day is related to that in the Central

Plains, but new forms have developed after blending with local customs.

All in all, the particular Double Seventh Day customs observed in Guangdong province are the result of repeated large-scale immigration of dominant families from the north to the south since the end of the Western Jin Dynasty when the Central Plains were in chaos. The customs were blended, altered and consolidated along the way, keeping some features of the northern area which can be traced back to as early as the Five Dynasties. However, they were obviously influenced by upper-class lifestyle rather than that of the lower class.

Of course, the spread of Qiqiao customs can not be attributed to the Hakka people alone, who acted as only one of the many powers in the process of long-distance diffusion. Under the rule of united and centralized reigns like the Han, Tang, Ming and Qing Dynasties, people migrated from place to place out of reasons such as doing business filling, official duty or family reunion. Similarly, in turbulent times people migrated to flee from wars and chaos. The continuous mobility of population contributed to the slow, periodical spread of culture and customs. Literary works also play a significant role in this momentum. During the spread, the customs evolved in their own way, adapting to new natural environment, economic conditions and local customs. Influenced by all these elements, they gradually transformed into folk customs with distinguishing characteristics.

Double Seventh Day in Guangdong is not only a festival but also a reminder of important historical events and stages of cultural exchange between different ethnic groups resulted from the former. It bears a witness to the shared history of ancient Chinese of different ethnicities who contributed to the opening up of frontiers, to which we should pay due attention in future study.

Chapter V
The History and Forms of Qixi Celebrations

Section 1   The Double Seventh Celebrations Involving Working Women

Since the emergence of the folk story "The Cowherd and the Weaver Fairy", the couple has been regarded as the representatives of ordinary Chinese farmers, with husbands ploughing and wives weaving to support their family. Therefore, the Cowherd is entrusted with the task of providing food for the dinning table, while the Weaver Fairy is responsible for clothing. In some places, the Weaver Fairy was gradually idolized as a goddess who is in charge of weaving and spinning.

The first topic we should discuss here is the sacrificial rites associated with loom-worship, which was sponsored by the Royal Bureau of Weaving and Dying of the Tang Dynasty (唐代宫廷织染署). This bureau oversaw weaving and dying affairs for the Tang royal court. According to "The Profiling of Administrative Organizations" in *The Book of the Tang Dynasty* (*Tangshu*,《唐书·百官志》): "The Bureau of Weaving and Dying conducts sacrificial rite of Loom-worshiping on the Double Seventh." As the loom is worshiped as an embodiment of the Weaving Goddess, the timing of sacrificial rites on the Double Seventh suggests a obvious connection with the folk story.

While the ladies of wealthy and official families celebrated the day with feasting, offering affluent sacrifices and joyful get-together, working women of poor families observed it through weaving and spinning. According to a quotation from the annals of Hubei and Hunan in "The Festive Customs" from *An Extensive Collection of Literature of All Times* (*Gujin Tushu Jicheng*,《古今图书集成·岁功典》), in Yingshan county (now Guangshui city of Hubei province), "[f]or poor women, it is a tradition to weave and spin instead of conducting festive celebrations on Double Seventh Day, while the gentry would propose a toast on the day." Celebrating the festival through spinning and weaving is the most original way to observe the day, if we take the image of the Weaver Fairy in the folk story into consideration. For women, the underlying philosophy is pursuing happiness and wealth through their own work instead of relying on somebody else, which in feudal China usually meant one's parents or husband. This custom embodies exactly the theme of the folk story, and with richer implications.

Another similar custom allowed women to gather on the evening of lunar July 7th to do needlework together. They would exchange their needlework on such get-togethers for appraisal, mutual learning and comparison. According to quotations from the annals of Shandong in "The Festive Customs" from *An Extensive Collection of Literature of All Times*, in Tangyi county, "On lunar July 7th, women engage themselves in needlework competitions as part of the Qiqiao celebrations. Noodles are served and consumed for good luck."

In feudal China, cooking was regarded another important skill a qualified housewife should command. In many regions of nothern China, cooking various wheaten foods on Double Seventh Day is

another significant way to observe it. In some cases, girls compete with each other in making flour delicacies that are both good to see and eat.

The folk story "The Cowherd and the Weaver Fairy" expressed the working people's desire for a happy life in ancient China, so the Double Seventh should be celebrated as a festival for working people. But, due to the limited means of farming families and the fact that they usually lived in scattered villages in extensive rural area, it was hard for them to hold large-scale festive activities. Instead, activities such as weaving under a crescent moon, story-telling in small circles, fortune-telling with bean sprouts in water basins, or observing floating clouds around the Milky Way became better options and the main forms of their Double Seventh celebrations. In this sense, these activities were conducted on a more extensive population base, and were more meaningful than those conducted in rich families, though seemingly in want of a joyful festive atmosphere.

The emotional impact of the folk story, which had been a part of Chinese collective memory since the Warring States period, had a far-reaching influence on people's lives. In the Qin Dynasty, auspicious days fit for weddings were designated in some almanacs based on their connection with the folk story. A bridge was built over the Wei River at the capital of the Qin Dynasty to mimic the one over the Milky Way mentioned in the folk story according to *Sanfu Huangtu*. These facts demonstrate that some of the plots in the story were actualized over 2000 years ago, proving its truth and promoting its popularity.

Meanwhile, the spirit of pursuing marital freedom and a happy

七夕文化透视 ▸▸▸
The Cowherd and the Weaver Fairy
A Study on the Folk Story and Double Seventh Day

life as well as virtues such as diligence, chastity in marriage and pure love embodied by the hero and the heroine were highly valued among working people. The belief that the couple had the power to fulfil one's dreams initiated sacrificial rites and celebrant activities. Despite the ruling class's attempts to dilute, replace or even cover up the rebellious theme of the folk story, it remained immensely popular among ordinary people. The images of the Cowherd and the Weaver Fairy were continuously reinforced through generations as the result of retelling, gradually establishing Double Seventh Day as an important folk festival in China.

Section 2   A Summing-up of Popular Ways of Qiqiao Celebrations

As a manifestation of ancient Chinese culture, the folk story "The Cowherd and the Weaver Fairy" at the meantime profiled the development of ancient Chinese society. The conflict between folk and elite cultures, as well as the eventual compromise through inter-class social contact, finally limited the theme of the Double Seventh celebrations to Qiqiao activities such as praying for blessings on one's needlework skills and marital life, instead of its original anti-feudal theme among women.

Although Double Seventh Day is primarily celebrated among unmarried girls in many places of China, in some other areas, it is celebrated on a broader basis by all women, varying in purposes and celebrant forms. For example, the needle-threading competition, which was discussed in Section 1, allows the participation of all

women, old and young, in a family. It is actually a perfect occasion for skill-imparting and experience-sharing, especially in needlework, which was regarded as the priority expertise expected of a qualified wife. From the earliest record on the festival during the Han Dynasty all the way down to the Song Dynasty of the Southern and Northern Dynasties, essays, poems and literary sketches written on the festival mostly focused on the imagined reunion of the couple. It was not until the Qi and Liang of Southern and Northern Dynasties that people started to shift their attention to Qiqiao celebrations. The reason for it is that the spread and popularization of a festival takes time.

Since the Southern and Northern Dynasties, diverse Double Seventh festive celebrations, which varied from place to place and changed over time, have been recorded in numerous pieces of literature, expressing the desires and longings of people from all walks of society. They are very helpful in introducing us to the rich entailment of the festival. Although some of these celebrations have been mentioned in previous sections, a summing-up will still be provided here.

I. Needle-threading activity

According to relevant accounts found in *A Miscellaneous Work from Chang'an* and *Festivals and Folk Customs of Jing and Chu Area*, "Threading 7 needle eyes on Double Seventh Day" meant to mark the day with the number "seven". The practice underwent changes in the following dynasties. As was recorded in *A Memoir on Kaiyuan and Tianbao Years of the Tang Dynasty* (*Kaiyuan Tianbao Yishi*,《开元天宝遗事》), it was a fashion for court ladies "to thread 9 needle eyes under the moonlight with silk threads of 5 colors", as the combination of 5 (colors) and 9 (needle eyes) makes 14, which represents "double 7". During the Southern and Northern Dynasties, there was a practice of "threading 2 needle eyes", as was also recorded in several poems from that period. From these poems, we can infer that "threading 2 needle eyes" means putting two needles together to create two eyes for threading. Therefore, it was similar to "threading 7 needle eyes or 9 needle eyes" (either holding them or piercing them onto some fabric in parallel). But why "2 needle eyes"? Probably because the combination of 2 and 5 (colors of silk threads used in threading) makes 7. Many poems dedicated to this custom support the interpretation. However, in some other poems such as "Ode on Double Seventh Eve" (《七夕赋》) by Yu Xin, reads: "The tightly braided silk strands go through the needle eye, which was tiny and hollow inside", there was no mention of the number of needle eyes. It is also the case with several other poems. So it seems that there may not have been a specific requirement regarding the number of needle-eyes in folk practice. But still, the needle eyes used in Qiqiao activities were supposed to be as tiny as possible, as delicate embroidery product required smaller needles and thinner silk threads.

Court ladies, instead, didn't spend much time on embroidery, as there were professional embroiderers in the royal court to do the work. It would be a challenge for them to thread extremely thin needles. To accomodate this, they made up for that by increasing the number of needle eyes. According to *The Collated Records on Peking's History and Culture* (*Rixia Jiuwen Kao*, 《日下旧闻考》) by Dou Guangding and Zhu Yun, court ladies and their maids would

ascend Jiuyin Terrace on the day to "thread 9 needle eyes with silk thread strands of 5 colors. Those who got the job done in the shortest time were considered the 'winners of Qiao' (believed to be blessed with needlework skills and good luck), while others were the 'losers of Qiao'". The continuation of court rites is obvious. This aristocratic practice was later adopted by people outside the royal quarters and became a routine in folk celebrations of some places. As for the general "needle-threading" custom, an interesting phenomenon is the coexistence of all varied practices from different times and places, which contributes to the formation of a colorful Qiqiao culture. In the poem "Double Seventh Eve" by Cui Hao of the Tang Dynasty, the poet wrote: "Under the silvery moonlight streaming down, every girl is busy with their needle and thread in town (Chang'an city)." This is a proof of the popularity of needle-threading competitions as an important festive activity on this evening.

According to *A Miscellaneous Work from Chang'an*, "court ladies and their maids celebrated the festival on Kaijin Pavillion to get closer to the moon", so surely Qiqiao activities were conducted under the moonlight. The custom was upheld by royal courts during the Wei, Jin, Southern and Northern Dynasties. Numerous historical resources from the Southern Dynasties as well as the Tang and Yuan Dynasties recorded the event as "threading needles on high rise pavilions under the moon". It is obvious that the rite was supposed to take place in the open air. From what has been discussed above, we can see that needle-threading is an age-old Qiqiao activity of great popularity observed as late as in modern times.

七夕文化透视 ▸▸▸
The Cowherd and the Weaver Fairy
A Study on the Folk Story and Double Seventh Day

Figure 15 Praying for Blessings through Needle–threading

by Lu Haiyan

II. Qiqiao with bean and wheat sprouts

Bean and wheat were the staple foods in ancient China and the foundation of the country was built on agriculture. Girls were taught to learn the importance of farming and cultivation by nurturing bean and wheat seeds in bowls filled with clean water till they germinate. The practice of nurturing these seeds before Double Seventh Day was an important process to acquire agricultural expertise and learn about knowledge of plant-growing. From the Weaver Fairy's perspective, we can regard the festival as a prayer for good needlework skills, but from that of the Cowherd's, it signifies a prayer for a good harvest. According to volume 8 titled "Double Seventh Day of Folk Customs" in *Records of Folk Customs in Kaifeng the East Capital* by Meng Yuanlao of the Song Dynasty, long before the day on which the festival falls:

> [Girls] would put green beans, red beans and wheat grains in a china bowl filled with water. Several days later, when sprouts of several inches long appeared, the grower would tie them up in small bundles, lovingly calling them "New Sprouts".

In other literary or historical accounts, it is also called "Wu Sheng" (五生), meaning "sprouts of crops" symbolizing a wish for good and strong crop stalks. Casting the bean and wheat sprouts into a water basin to do fortune-telling about the grower's marriage and future by deciphering the shadows on the bottom of the basin

七夕文化透视 ▸▸▸
The Cowherd and the Weaver Fairy
A Study on the Folk Story and Double Seventh Day

is a game which brought girls imagination into full play. They would do it again and again, making new predictions each time to express their longings for the future freely. The long process of seed picking, grain soaking, germinating and daily water changing usually starts a month before the festival, calling for patience and perserverence. It is also a test on the grower's agricultural expertise, thus greatly lengthened the festival. In many regions, the sprouts are called "Qiao sprouts" (巧芽), which means "sprouts that show your deftness and will bring you good luck". The sprouts, which are usually tied up in small bundles with colorful silk threads, are offered as a sacrifice in front of a painting or model of Queen Qiao.

Praying for blessings from fairies by deciphering the sprout shadows is very popular in Qiqiao celebrations conducted in northern China. In many cases, the shadows that look like needles or soles are considered the best, as they prove that the sprout grower is adored by Queen Qiao and will excel in needlework and be blessed with happiness.

In some places, the participation of young married women is allowed in celebrations, but only in a particular form—soothsaying on the gender of an unborn offspring or praying for pregnancy. Although already deviated from its original theme of lovers' reunion, the festive variations concerning different aspects of family life which are ethical and helpful are quite understandable when taking its popularity in society into consideration.

会餐 败办卜巧

Figure 16　Dinner Party

by Lu Haiyan

七夕文化透视 ▸▸▸
The Cowherd and the Weaver Fairy
A Study on the Folk Story and Double Seventh Day

III. Qiqiao by floating needles in water

An account of the Double Seventh Qiqiao events in *The Ways and Folk Customs in the Capital* (*Dijing Jingwu Lüe*,《帝京景物略》) by Yu Yizheng and Liu Dong of the Ming Dynasty is quoted as follows:

> Needle floating takes place at noon on lunar July 7th. Girls and young wives expose a basin of water under the sun. A while later, when a thin layer of dust film has formed on the surface of the water, they cast embroidery needles onto it in the hope that it will hold up the needles. If the shadows cast on the bottom of the basin by the bunch of needles look like cloud patterns, flowers, animals, birds, soles or scissors, the owner of the needles will be congratulated as the winner of "Qiao", who is believed to be blessed with deft hands.

This practice was recorded in many other historical resources from the Ming and Qing Dynasties. Exposing a water basin under the sun allows the material of light density to rise onto the surface of the water and form a thin layer of film along with the dust that has fallen into the water. The shadows cast by the needle bunches and the fine material attached around them on the basin's bottom are judged. This was another type of Qiqiao activity, but was too simple and straightforward to leave much room for imagination and entertainment. In some places, it was practiced along with needle-threading. Different from other Qiqiao games, needle-floating, which is easier to conduct under the sun, would be a real challenge in the evening. The thin film formed on the water surface would be damaged so easily that it's always very difficult to hold up the

needles after repeated attempts. As a result, another variety of the custom was developed. During the Qing Dynasty, pine needles which are lighter and more changeable in size and shape replaced steel needles in the ritual. This enabled the formation of more diversified patterns in the water.

IV. Qiqiao with cobweb

According to *The Festivals and Folk Customs of the Jing and Chu Area*, during the Southern and Northern Dynasties, there was a custom of "offering fruits and melons on desks in the courtyard for Queen Qiao. Auspicious it was believed to have a cobweb spun on those fruits and melons." As spiders always dangle themselves down along a thin thread unexpectedly, they are believed to be messengers from God to bring you good luck. They are affectionately nicknamed "good luck darlings" (喜子). In "Vulgar Names" from *New Discussions* (*Xinlun*, 《新论·鄙名篇》), Liu Zhou of the Northern Qi Dynasty wrote: "Now ignorant men and women take spiders coming their way in daylight as an auspicious sign of an up-coming good streak of luck." Many other literary works supported this ancient idea. Spiders are good at knitting and weaving, so ancient women took them as an oracle to determine whether or not they were blessed by Queen Qiao with expertise and wisdom. This custom continued until the Qing Dynasty. Similar accounts can be found in other resources such as "The Festive Customs" in *An Extensive Collection of Literature of All Times*.

The presence of cobwebs on fruits and melons was only one way to judge whether one was blessed or not. In some other cases, people took an active initiative in "letting it happen" instead of "waiting for gains without pains". Girls started searching high and low for cobwebs on looms and flowers, or they exhausted every corner of their house to get as many spiders as possible in order to make sure that they were blessed. However, in wealthy or aristocratic families where the houses were well-maintained and regularly cleaned, cobwebs were rare. The girls then figured out another way to ensure they "are blessed". They put captured spiders into a box to see whether they spin webs or not. It was recorded in "Qiqiao Pavillion" in *A Memoir on Kaiyuan and Tianbao years of Tang Dynasty* that court ladies and their maids would "capture spiders and put them into a small box on July 7th. At dawn, the box would be opened and the density of the cobweb would be taken as a standard to go by in judging whether the owner was blessed by Queen Qiao or not. If the cobweb was densely spun, the owner was a darling; if not, she was not much favored by Queen Qiao. The practice gradually popularized in the whole society." In volume 3 of *A Miscellaneous Records of History* (*Wuling Jiushi*,《武林旧事》), it was recorded that during the Southern Song Dynasty, on lunar July 7th, "waxen birds were floated in water basins. Girls and housewives competed in threading needles under the moonlight, enjoying themselves drinking and eating. They also put small spiders in boxes, praying for the spiders to spin dense cobwebs to ensure their blessings from Queen Qiao." From this we can see that cobwebs were widely and diversely used in Qiqiao activities.

V. Making predictions about crop harvest through the observation of cloud patterns

A quotation from *The Annals of Henan* (《河南志书》) in *An Extensive Collection of Literature of All Times: The Festive Customs* goes like this: "[In Jixian county,] on the evening of lunar July 7th, people kneel down to pray for good luck if they see white cloud in the Milky Way."

Another quotation from *The Annals of Jiangnan Area* reads: "On lunar July 7th in Tongzhou, women look into the sky for rosy clouds which are believed to be an oracle from Queen Qiao, indicating one is blessed or not." A quotation from *A Collection of Strange Stories* (《杂异书》) in volume 31 of *Imperial Readings of the Taiping Era* reads:

> It is believed that the Gate to Heaven opens up on the evening of lunar July 7th. It was said that there was once a young girl who insisted on staying indoors while her family went out to witness the magical view. When questioned, she said: "If you are destined to witness the sight of wonder, you will be able to see it whether you are indoors or outdoors." In the depth of the night, the wonder did occur, and she saw it.

Other resources also recorded the observance of this custom during the Tang and Song Dynasties, in which the rosy clouds carrying the Cowherd and the Weaver Fairy on their way to their meeting place, or the opening of the Heavenly Gate, which is usually believed to be marked by brilliant and dazzling array of colors across the sky like in fairy tales, are regarded as auspicious signs heralding something good.

The origin of this custom can be attributed to two customs: one is looking at Vega and Altair as well as the Milky Way during prayers on the evening of July 7th; the other is the ancient practice of making predictions about natural disasters and crop harvest through the observation of cloud patterns in the sky. In *The Rites of Zhou* (*Zhouli*,《周礼》), there is a sentence that reads "Making predictions on natural disasters and crop harvest by interpreting auspicious and ominous signs hidden in cloud patterns." This proves that the custom can be traced back to an early time. It was combined with Qiqiao customs in its process of circulation. Zhou Chu of the Jin Dynasty already recorded in his *The Records of Regional Folk Customs* the custom of observing cloud patterns around the Milky Way on the tradition of July 7th. The author of "The Festive Customs" in *An Extensive Collection of Literature of All Times* quoted from *Annals of Jiangnan Area*: "[In Gaoyou of Jiangsu province,] before July 7th, people observe the Milky Way to make predictions about the harvest in the following year." In Taihu county, "On July 7th, people make predictions about grain price based on the distance between the Milky Way and the port." *The Annals of Jiangxi* also recorded a similar custom in Qianshan county.

The custom of using cobwebs in Qiqiao activities and making predictions about crop harvest through the observation of cloud patterns expanded the population involved in Qiqiao activities. It extended from unmarried girls to married women and men, because peasants, especially experienced ones who are concerned about the harvest in upcoming year, are usually males advanced in years. The festival was thus bestowed with much richer connotations. As for intellectuals, they readily attached their personal emotions or life experiences to the day or the weather conditions of the day when criticizing corruption and injustice in the current administration, expressing their sadness at being separated from their loved ones, or voicing their longing for family reunions. Literary works of this type abounded in history.

Among the poems about lunar July 7th which extol loyalty in love, "Magpie-bridge Fairy" (《鹊桥仙》) by Qin Guan from the Song Dynasty is a classic. Though farming and harvesting played a part in Qiqiao activities, they were rarely mentioned in

poems, most probably because that reading and writing, let along poem composing, were luxury activities that peasants in feudal China could not afford. Anyway, the involvement of intellectuals and peasants in the folk festival greatly enriched its forms and connotation.

VI. Qiqiao by storing water on July 7th in southern China

According to a quotation from *The Annals of Jiangxi* in *An Extensive Collection of Literature of All Times: The Festive Customs*, in Guangchang county:

> On July 7th, girls and housewives gather under the moon to engage in Qiqiao. They kneel down and pray, then leave honey water with fruit bits in the courtyard overnight and drink it first thing in the morning. The honey water called "water of Qiao" is believed to bring good luck and superior expertise in needlework.

The origin of this custom can be traced back to the tradition of admiring Milky Way and listening to the chattering of its water at night, with a hope for a smooth reunion of the couple on July 7th. Placing a basin of water (similar to the northern practice of germinating bean or wheat sprouts in bowls or basins) in open air overnight expresses people's goodwill in capturing water from the Milky Way. The regional variations in ceremonial details show the localization of the customs when they were popularized. Generally speaking, this day remains a festival for women and children.

七夕文化透视 ▶▶▶
The Cowherd and the Weaver Fairy
A Study on the Folk Story and Double Seventh Day

VII. Qiqiao with writing brushes, ink holders and essays

In feudal China, formal education was exclusively intended for boys, though girls from wealthy families, especially those of officials' received home-schooling in writing, chess-playing and artistic performance. It was not until modern times when women started to enjoy higher social status and feudal ethics such as strict prohibition on contact between men and women slackened, if not completely given up, that activities concerning reading and writing assumed a more important role in Qiqiao celebrations. Some historical and literary resources describe the event as one in which both men and women, including children, took part in essay-writing competitions. Volume 8 of *The Records of Folk Customs in Kaifeng the East Capital* recorded Qiqiao activities conducted in privileged families in the Central Plains as follows:

> On the evening of lunar July 6th and 7th, various objects for the Qiqiao rite are displayed, including "writing brushes and ink holders for children to compete in poem composition" while girls present their hand-made artifacts.

A quotation from *The Annals of Fujian* in *An Extensive Collection of Literature of All Times: The Festive Customs* records a folk practice conducted in Changting county as: "On the morning of July 7th, pupils from local schools chant poems loudly while beating drums. They hang paper gourds on bamboo sticks and burn their homework papers outside the school to Qiqiao (praying for good academic performance)". This shows that the rite is open unexceptionally to students, male or female, to satisfy their desire for better academic performance. Different from other Qiqiao activities, this one was primarily, though not exclusively, meant for young intellectuals and children. Children are closely related with women, their main care-giver, with whom they spend more time than anyone else when they are young. Young intellectuals, on the other hand, are at a stage of life in which they are naturally attracted to young women who share similar mindset or psychological state being. Furthermore, essay-writing competition is a perfect way to highlight their academic gift so as to attract attention from the opposite gender.

In some areas, Qiqiao games are combined with sacrificial and worship rites dedicated to Vega, also known as Queen Qiao (the Weaver Fairy). The forms and scale of this combination as well as the importance people attach to the rites vary from place to place, but together they constitute the rich and colorful Qiqiao culture in China. Generally speaking, the rite is conducted more ceremoniously in the north, where it keeps a more antique flavour in reference to ancient records, while in the south more or less adapted or localized versions of the tradition exist. Furthermore, Qiqiao, as a festive activity, is intended for unmarried juvenile girls in the north, while in the south, although girls remain the primary participants, married female adult women and men, especially young intellectuals, also get involved in different ways. Anyway, one thing is clear: rich customs and stories about July 7th, or Double Seventh Day, have been developed all over the country. Due to the interference from the ruling class, the ethical teachings of feudal scholars and moralists (including patriarchs in influential families), the day which had intended to honor the reunion between the star-crossed lovers "the Cowherd" and "the Weaver Fairy" finally evolved into one praying for good luck in marriage

七夕文化透视 ▸▸▸
The Cowherd and the Weaver Fairy
A Study on the Folk Story and Double Seventh Day

and outstanding needlework skills. It has become a festive occasion for feasts and joyful get-togethers among high-class women. But still, some young people continued to observe the day in harmony with its original connotation by praying while looking at the Milky Way in the evening or worshiping the couple under the moonlight. The celebrations among the masses, though in some degree subject to the influence of feudal ethics and main-stream culture of their time, were mostly related to agricultural production and their daily life, expressing the desires of ordinary people, especially young men and women. All in all, the fact that chastity in love remains the most important theme in the folk story "The Cowherd and the Weaver Fairy" is undoubtable, as has been illustrated by numerous articles and poems.

On July 7th, a schedule crammed with gatherings, sharing and competitions in various domestic skills including cooking, artifact making, weaving and embroidering not only promoted the tranmission of traditional expertise, but also improved women's life skills. It was also an occasion for socialization and knowledge transmission between juvenile girls, where they practiced organizational and leadership skills, cultivated their spirit of cooperation and teamwork as well as developed their ability to accomplish tasks. In this sense, we can say that the festival, despite the pressure from the feudal ruling class and the mainstream culture, played a positive role in women's education in feudal China. It served as an important self-run, self-taught workshop where elders tutored youth, new hands apprenticed themselves to experienced ones from generation to generation.

Either worshiping the Weaver Fairy as the goddess in charge of weaving and embroidery affairs through offeringss, prayers or

staying up overnight weaving, spinning or paying respects to the Cowherd as the god in charge of agricultural production, making predictions about the up-coning year's harvest, especially about weather conditions or grain price in upcoming year through reading cloud-patterns on the evening of July 7th is a popular traditional practice. The two figures which represent numerous ordinary working couples in feudal agricultural Chinese society play their part in providing moral support and comfort for the masses. The limited ancient literature, though not abundant in number, reveals the desires and longings of peasants in the past.

The rich and diverse festive customs about Double Seventh Day reflect the differences in taste, preferences, age, social status, gender and geographical conditions among celebrants in the process of its spread. Kids are interested in joyful gatherings with delicacies and games like Qiqiao with cobwebs. Young men and women are more concerned about their future, in the former case more focused on their academic performance, while in the latter case emphasizing superior needlework abilities and a good marriage. Middle-aged males are worried about professional promotion or obsessed with loneliness when they pursue their career development away from their families. The elders in rural areas are more concerned about the harvest next year while intellectuals reflect on the ups and downs in their pursuit of ambition fulfillment. Thus, a probe into Qiqiao customs and ways of celebrations on Double Seventh Day provides us with a convenient way to learn about social condition and collective psychology in ancient times. The transformation of the festive customs has been ongoing from the very beginning. Through studying the differences in customs and ways of celebrations between aristocratic classes and grassroots, and on interactions and mutual

七夕文化透视 ▶▶▶
The Cowherd and the Weaver Fairy
A Study on the Folk Story and Double Seventh Day

influence that occured during the evolutionary process, we can gain a better perspective on the influence of feudal ethics and the ideology of the ruling class on people's lives and cognition. Additionally, the efforts made by ordinary people to express their longings and wishes in a indirect manner despite social constraints can be studied, too.

Section 3   The Qiqiao Customs Concerning Women and Youth at Marriageable Age

I. Girls and married young women dying their nails red with petals of garden balsam

Quoting from *The Annals of Jiangnan*, an account in "The Festive Customs" in *An Extensive Collection of Literature of All Times* reads as follows:

> [In Wujin county,] on July 7th, women collected petals of garden balsam to dye their nails red. They then worship Vega, the goddess in charge of weaving and embroidery affairs, in the Qiqiao ritual.

This custom is still practiced today in many provinces in the north. Two seemingly unrelated practices are somehow connected in this case. The purpose of the Qiqiao ritual is to pray for skillful and nimble hands. Dying the nails in a beautiful color not only highlights the role of hands in working and socializing, but also serve as a manifestation of the dyer's taste and dexterity. It is such a meticulous task that requires patience and expertise involving determining the right shade of color, ensuring the deepest shade being applied in the

right position (as in common practice, only a small upper middle sphere of each nail should be dyed bright red while leaving the color to fade off in surrounding area), and preventing the color from spilling out over the nail edge, etc. As nails are small and wrapped up after dying to let the color stay, the whole process calls for high dexterity and good aesthetic taste. In the past, girls and young housewives in northwestern China and the Central Plains would start dying their nails by the end of lunar June. In Longnan and Tianshui cities of Gansu province, a "welcome ritual for Queen Qiao is conducted on June 30th. In the following sacrificial and competitive activities in the Qiqiao rites which last for 7 days and 8 nights, young girls show and compare their beautifully dyed nails for appraisal as another form of competition during the festival.

During the summer, Garden balsam blossoms. With petals scarlet and juicy, it is a perfect material for nail dying. In volume 1 of *A Sequel to Miscellaneous Notes from Guixin Street of Ling'an* (*Guixin Zashi Xuji*,《癸辛杂识续集上》) by Zhou Mi of the Southern Song Dynasty, there is an entry titled "Nail-dying with garden balsam" that suggests the following procedure:

> Pick the brightest red garden balsam petals. Crush them and mix with alum. Polish the nails and apply the mixed paste onto them, then wrap the nails with clean cloth. Leave the cloth-wrapped nails that way overnight. After the first dye, the nails will only be light red, but the shade will deepen after several times' redye and eventually turn into beautiful bright red.

七夕文化透视 ▸▸▸
The Cowherd and the Weaver Fairy
A Study on the Folk Story and Double Seventh Day

This proves the long history of the custom which could be traced back at least to the Southern Song Dynasty.

A further discussion on the name of garden balsam, which in Chinese means "the flower of Fairy Phoenix", might be necessary.

It is academically acknowledged that the ancient Qin people took phoenix as their totem. The story about Nüxiu, a female descendant of Emperor Zhuanxu, who gulped down a swallow's egg before giving birth to Daye, the ancestor of the Qin people, is recorded in "The History of Qin" in *Records of the Grand Historian*. This is the earliest historical literature mentioning the origin of the totem worship. It is also mentioned that Dafei, the son of Daye, assisted Emperor Shun in improving geographical conditions and taming of wild animals, thus was conferred the family name "Ying" (嬴) by the Emperor. The particular totem-worship is also reflected in *The Classic of Mountains and Seas: Inland Part* as a fairy tale, stating: "The ying people stand with bird-like claws." Many other resources from ancient times reveal the connection between the Qin people and their totem, the Phoenix. Many officials in the Qin court took on names involving the phoenix and other birds. The connection between the name "the flower of Fairy Phoenix" which plays a part on Double Seventh Day and the Weaver Fairy to whom the festival is dedicated suggests the relevance of the Qin people to the Weaver Fairy. It might be a remnant of ancient collective memory.

In Longnan and Tianshui cities in Gansu province, the mountains named "Phoenix" are numerous, possibly another indication of the ancient memory about totem worship and sacrificial rituals of the Qin people. Taking Mountain Phoenix of Changdao, a town which is very near to Mountain Dabuzi, as an example. A

stone tablet carved with "last forever" was erected during the Tianqi period of the Ming Dynasty (1621-1627). Worshiped in the temple on top of the mountain are the statues of Goddess Vega (the Weaver Fairy) and Queen Nüwa, the ancestor of the Chinese. The temple was destroyed in an earthquake in the winter of 1440, but was rebuilt later. In the Qing Dynasty, two other stone tablets were erected respectively in 1731 and 1742. The former was inscribed with an introduction to the mountain history and the Chinese characters on the latter read: "Be happily united in marriage". There is another mountain named Phoenix to the west of Xihe county with the neighborhood adjoining it named "village phoenix". There is also an age-old castle on top of the mountain nicknamed by the locals as "the city of phoenix". Further to the west of Xihe county, there is still another mountain phoenix quite near to Lixian county.

Mountains named as Phoenix are so numerous in important counties such as Chengxian, Huixian, Wudu and Tanchang in Gansu province that abundant literary and history records were written about them.

It is a popular practice for families with girls or young housewives in Longnan and Tianshui cities to plant garden balsam in their courtyard. It gives the quarters a special lively air. The girls and housewives showcase and compare their beautiful nails at their routine needlework gatherings. This has become a special part of the Qiqiao activities in Double Seventh Day celebrations.

II. Beautifying facial skins and getting rid of moles, scars, freckles, acne and other skin disorders on July 7th

The mysterious and festive atmosphere of Double Seventh Day and its connection to immortals in Heaven convince the young

七夕文化透视 ▶▶▶
The Cowherd and the Weaver Fairy
A Study on the Folk Story and Double Seventh Day

people, both men and women, that they can get rid of annoying skin disorders on the day and better their looking.

In *An Exhaustive Records of Mystic Techniques by Huainan Zi* (*Huainan Wanbi Shu*,《淮南万毕术》), there is the following account:

> At noon on July 7th, pick 7 leaves from melon vines and go into the northern Hall. Stand facing south and rub your face with the leaves for a while, then you will have a face rid of speckles and moles.

This method is also quoted in *Imperial Readings of the Taiping Era* and *Compendium of Materia Medica* (*Bencao Gangmu*,《本草纲目》, a book on Chinese herbal medicine). Taking advantage of the festival's popularity, sorcerers claimed that melon leaves picked on the particular day have amazing effects on moles and speckles. During early autumn, when plant leaves are ripened, it's possible that the rich juice from melon leaves may work in some way in treating skin disorders, but its effect was so exaggerated and the process so absurd and mysterious that it's unbelievable for modern readers.

In volume 31 of *Imperial Readings of the Taiping Era*, a quotation from *Monthly Records by Madame Wei* (*Weishi Yuelu*,《韦氏月录》) states:

> Take some blood from a black-bone chicken on lunar July 7th, and mix it with crushed petals of peach blossoms which were picked on lunar March 3rd. Smear the paste all over your face and body. Repeat it 2 to 3 times daily in a row, you will get a fair and silky complexion with the brilliance of jade. This secret formula was tried by Princess Taiping of the Tang

Dynasty, and it worked amazingly.

An item in *Suggestions on Regimen* (*Zunsheng Bajian*,《遵生八笺》) reads:

> Pick sesame blossoms on lunar July 7th, dry them in the shade before crushing them into powder, and put them into sesame oil. Apply the mixture to your eye-brows, and new brow hair will grow.
>
> Take roots from a lily bulb on lunar July 7th, crush them completely. Then put them in a new clean pottery drying in the shade for 100 days. Smear your scalp where white hairs have been newly pulled, and the dark ones will grow soon.
>
> Take a box of bee pupae on lunar July 7th, dry them up, crush them into powder, and mix up with honey. Apply the mixture to your face and it can get rid of speckles.
>
> Take 14 fireflies on lunar July 7th and rub them on your hair. The hair will turn black soon.

According to an account in *The Annals of Jiangnan* which was quoted in volume 65 of "The Festive Customs" in *An Extensive Collection of Literature of All Times*:

> In Wuxi county of Jiangsu province, on the evening of lunar July 7th, girls immerse petals of different flowers into morning dew and air them in the courtyard. On the following morning, they wash their face with the mixed liquid. It is believed to work well on bettering your complexion.

七夕文化透视 ▸▸▸
The Cowherd and the Weaver Fairy
A Study on the Folk Story and Double Seventh Day

In *The Annals of Zhejiang*, a custom in Taizhou prefecture is described:

> [For women to] put a basin of water with petals in the open air to pray for blessings from the Weaver Fairy, Queen Qiao. The following morning, girls wash and comb their hair with the water.

Still, it was believed that water blessed by Queen Qiao on July 7th would give people good looks. In Kaihua county of Zhejiang, there is a custom "for young boys and girls to wash their hair with water mixed with crushed hibiscus leaves on the morning of July 7th". In Suichang county, "on lunar July 7th, children wash their hair in a river. Girls celebrate the day with Qiqiao activities." According to *Annals of Fujian*, in Xintian county, "on the early morning of July 7th, children let down their hair and go to the grasses for the moisture of morning dew. It is believed that hair will grow dark and long if this is done." In *The Annals of Guangdong*, it is recorded that in Yingde county:

> Beside the star Vega, there is a minor star in charge of maiden affairs. Girls and young housewives would stay up late till the depths of the night, burn incense and pray. It is believed that the minor star will bless the prayer with good look and fair complexion.

Since the Wei and Jin Dynasties, many influential families migrated from the north to the south, first to the Jiangnan area, then further to Guangdong and Fujian provinces after the collapse of the Southern dynasties and the Southern Song Dynasty consecutively. That is why in parts of Zhejiang and Guangdong, the Double Seventh, otherwise called the Qiqiao Festival, is still celebrated in a luxurious way which reveals its origin from a higher social class. The Qiqiao celebrations in these areas in general attach more importance to beauty treatments, suggesting the economic conditions and tastes of the participants. At the same time, customs popular in the north were brought to the south through different channels, as was recorded in a quotation from *The Annals of Huguang* in *An Extensive Collection of Literature of All Times: The Festive Customs*, where it states, "[In Youxian county,] women pick cypress leaves and peach twigs to boil water for hair-wash."

The pursuit of beauty is a human nature which is especially important for young people of marriageable age with a hope of impressing their peers of the opposite gender, especially those whom they take a liking to. They earnestly engage in beauty treatments. It's of vital importance for girls to look good at Qiqiao activities during festive celebrations where they get together, and compete with each other in every way. It is as important for boys to seek every chance to meet girls on the day. As in the folk story, the Weaver Fairy and the Cowherd got united in marriage out of their own will instead of being set up in an arranged marriage which had always been believed to be the only right ethical way in feudal China, the day enjoyed prestigious popularity among the youth who longed for freedom in love and marriage. This partly explains the magical power people attached onto the day in uniting young men and women in marriage.

III. Taking bath with the water blessed by the Weaver Fairy and the custom of rowing on the river

When the customs regarding Double Seventh Day were

七夕文化透视 ▸▸▸
The Cowherd and the Weaver Fairy
A Study on the Folk Story and Double Seventh Day

spread to Guagndong province where it is hot most of the time in a year, localization took place. At the beginning of lunar July, when other regions of the country, especially those in the north, were entering autumn and preparing for temperature drops, most parts of Guangdong province were still subject to unbearable heat. Another new type of custom concerning the festival then was developed: "taking a bath with water blessed by the Weaver Fairy, the daughter of the Jade Emperor". Qu Dajun recorded this at the beginning of the Qing Dynasty in "Customs and Events" of his *New Notes about Guangdong*:

> The Seventh Lady Day falls on lunar July 7th. It's a tradition to conduct Qiqiao activities and take a bath in water blessed by the Weaver Fairy on the day. People decorate the hull of the boat with Jasminum grandiflorum Linns and Jasmines while adorning the roof with kingfishers feathers. They then row on a river or a lake to mimic rowing in the Milky Way.

The so-called the Seventh Lady Day is actually Double Seventh Day, or the Qiqiao Festival, as it was and is still called in the north, as was discussed in previous chapters.

Zhang Hua wrote in his *Encyclopedic Records* (*Bowu Zhi*,《博物志》): "The Milky Way is connected with the sea." It was said that someone "rowed upstream all the way to the Milky Way and came across the famous couple there". The tradition in Guangdong of "rowing on a river or a lake" on Double Seventh Day is a reference to this story. Transplanting the story about the star-crossed couple onto one in which someone rowed all the way to the Milky Way diluted

its tragic theme in the same way as the transplanting of the story *"Dong Yong and the Seventh Fairy Lady"* onto Double Seventh Day. Of course, the need to take refuge from still unbearable hot in lunar July is another reason for the origin of the custom in Guangdong.

Section 4　Conducting Marital Ceremonies: Consulting Eight Characters for Horoscope and Conducting Engagement Ritual for the Bride and Bridegroom-to-be

"Consulting Eight Characters for horoscope" (问字) is an important step after the Marriage Proposal (提亲) in marriage preparations. The combination of eight characters which indicates the time of birth (believed to foretell a person's future) is consulted for preliminary confirmation of the marriage as an important ritual before the Engagement Ceremony (聘定). After the engagement, the girl is regarded as a member of her fiancé's family. In some high-brow families in feudal times, if a young man died before his wedding day, the girl would still be married into her in-laws' without a husband and live in widowhood for the rest of her life. From this we can see that "consulting eight characters" is a very important step in the establishment of a marital relationship.

According to a quotation from "The Festive Customs" in *The Annals of Henan* in *An Extensive Collection of Literature of All Times*, in Baishui county, "The families of potential bridegrooms compete in presenting festive gifts to the bride-to-be's on lunar July 7th. In some cases, the gifts were so lavish that they matched those given on the engagement ritual." According to *The Annals*

七夕文化透视 ▶▶▶
The Cowherd and the Weaver Fairy
A Study on the Folk Story and Double Seventh Day

of Huguang, it was a tradition in Xintian county "to conduct engagement and betrothal-gifts sending rituals (订婚纳彩) on luanr July 7th". The star-crossed couple were separated by the Milky Way and were allowed only one reunion once a year on lunar July 7th. Originally a tragic day, but later in its circulation with only the couple's reunion highlighted, the day was turned into a lucky occasion of matching young men and young women in marriage. In this sense the custom of conducting marital rituals on this day became established. Besides, the joyful get-togethers among girls in Qiqiao activities and the arranged encounters between young men and women which in some cases brought about beautiful results added to the festive atmosphere and made it a prefect day for conducting marital affairs.

Section 5　Worship and Praying to the Moon

Moon Worship is a popular custom among girls approaching marriageable age in southern China. It serves as a way to express their hopes for sweet love and harmonious marriage. In feudal China, marriages were typically arranged by parents, with the proposal coming from the bridegroom-to-be and his family to the bride-to-be and hers. It was considered rare and inappropriate for it to be done differently, especially for a young woman to this. Lunar July 7th was the only occasion for young girls to express their concerns on marital affairs and pray for blessings on their future marriages under the moon. Since on the evening of lunar July 7th, the moon is still a crescent, the custom was called "the worship of the crescent moon" (拜新月).

The custom, primarily observed in the area to the south of the Yangtze River, originated from the customs such as looking into the

night sky for Vega and Altar, watching the Milky Way in honor of the couple and making predictions about weather through reading cloud patterns on the evening of lunar July 7th.

All these customs were developed from, but still adhere to their original theme: "worshiping the Weaver Fairy and praying for blessings" on lunar July 7th. Other activities such as "Qiqiao" were actually a compromise between the desires of young women and the feudal ethics.

A group of participants exceptionally allowed in "the worship of the crescent moon" ritual were married women whose husbands were temporarily separated from them for some reason, such as pursuing education, serving in the army, or going on business trip. These wives would worship the moon praying for safe and quick return of their husbands. This is obviously a variation of the festive custom centered around "reunion" motif as manifested in the southern edition of the folk story in "the reunion of the couple on the magpie bridge over the Milky Way". The wives' love toward their husbands and their chastity in marriage which are expressed through the rite accord to the original theme of the festival.

Numerous ancient poems on this theme were written by poets mainly from Zhejiang, with a few exceptions from Jiangxi, Fujian and Anhui provinces. Shihui, the author of a famous Nanxi play (the Southern Opera) *The Moon-Worship Pavilion* (《拜月亭》) is a native to Hangzhou city. This indicates the geographical range within which the moon-worship custom is observed. On Double Seventh Day which marks at the beginning of autumn, it is still hot in the south. People enjoy the coolness of the outdoor night breeze, hence the orgination of the celebrations of Qiqiao rites such as "threading needles under the moonlight". As the moon is an eternal presence and witness to every

七夕文化透视 ▶▶▶
The Cowherd and the Weaver Fairy
A Study on the Folk Story and Double Seventh Day

ritual on this night, it has been eulogized in nearly all the ancient poems about the festival. That explains the relationship between moon-worship and the festival in honor of the couple, or to be exact, the Weaver Fairy.

What's special about the Moon-worship custom is that it is usually conducted alone, with no witnesses present when a girl spit out her inner most wishes and desire. This is different from the Qiqiao celebrations or the sacrificial rites conducted in groups in the north. In some cases, some adults pitch in to express their wishes for life.

Section 6   Germinating Bean Sprouts

If you want to Qiqiao with bean and wheat sprouts, you have to put carefully hand-picked bean or wheat grains beforehand into a basin full of clean water no later than mid-June, leaving at least half a month for them to sprout. First, you have to immerse the grains in warm water for a whole night so that the water can soak through. Then, you have to change to cold water and do it everyday till they grow long and good sprouts. This is a good test on the grower's carefulness, patience and sense of responsibility, a dry run for their participation in housework and agricultural labor in the future. The custom is still very popular in Longnan and Tianshui cities of Gansu province as well as in some other regions in the north.

In some places, "Germinating Sprouts for Qiqiao purpose" is called "growing five lives" (Zhong Wusheng, 种五生). Meng Yuanlao of the Song Dynasty wrote in his *Records of Folk Customs in Kaifeng the East Capital*:

Put beans or wheat grains into a china container to grow

sprouts. When they are several inches long, tie them up with silk strands of red and blue. It is called "growing five lives".

Bai Pu, a famous playwright of the Yuan Dynasty, wrote in act one of his drama *Drizzles on Chinese Parasol* (*Wutong Yu*,《梧桐雨》): "A small golden basin is growing five lives, which is served in front of a painting figuring the reunion of the Cowherd and the Weaver Fairy." The basin used for growing sprouts was called "basin of flowering lives", or the "basin of five lives" in ancient times. In "On July 7th" from *Notes on Customs around the Year in the Capital* (*Dijing Suishi Jisheng*,《帝京岁时纪盛·七夕》), the author Pan Yunbi of the Qing Dynasty wrote: "Several days before July 7th, girls grow wheat grains in small potteries to pay respects to Altair. The basin is called the 'basin growing five lives'." As the Cowherd star (Altair) represents hard-working peasants in feudal China, little girls are taught crop-growing skills in basins and potteries from an early age. Through yearly practice, they become more skillful in the work. During Qiqiao celebrations, girls take their sprouts to where the statue of Queen Qiao is seated for display and competition. They then use them in Qiqiao and Buqiao (卜巧 , an appraisal of their deftness) games. By lamplight (or under the moonlight in the south), sprouts are pinched into small pieces and thrown into water basin for appraisal of their deftness. This is a good exercise to boost the imagination and creative abilities of girls while also providing aesthetic education.

Section 7　Making Delicate Pastries as Sacrifice for Queen Qiao

Since the end of lunar June, girls are expected to start making

七夕文化透视 ▸▸▸
The Cowherd and the Weaver Fairy
A Study on the Folk Story and Double Seventh Day

pastries in the shape of fingered citron and chrysanthemum for sacrificial offering in front of Queen Qiao during the Double Seventh celebrations. It is actually another chance for girls to learn, to show, to exchange experiences and to compete in cooking with their peers. In ancient times, the appraisal of a girl's qualification whether she would make a good wife or not was mainly based on one hand in needlework skills including weaving, tailoring, sewing and embroidering, and on the other hand cooking. In northwestern China, it was referred to as "skills in preparing tea and meals". No wonder making delicate pastries is an important content in preparations for the Qiqiao Festival in the north. It was rather an occasion to acquire new cooking skills and put them into practice, then compare the products in a later competition than merely making preparations for the Qiqiao activity. Elder girls would do most of the work, while the younger ones served as assistants, watching and learning. The ones who outshined the others in cooking is regarded leaders and organizers of the Qiqiao ritual automatically, but would be replaced by younger ones if they got married the following year. There are naturally differences in ability and performance among the girls, just like what it is with academic performance which is closely related to family background and gift. In some families, girls started learning from their female elders at an early age, improving their skills step by step till they can do it independently.

The focus on pastry-making instead of dish-cooking on lunar July 7th reveals the fact that the activity "Competing for Qiao (deftness)" is more related to agricultural production in the north rather than cooking skills expected in feasts or business cuisine. The pastries to be offered to Queen Qiao on lunar July 7th should be "original" and "delicate" to show the creativity and deftness of the

maker. That is why the pastries, cold dishes and lotus roots are all supposed to be presented in beautiful patterns or shapes which called for dexterity in cutting, slicing, or pattern-setting. According to "On July 7th" in *An Extensive Collection of Literature of All Times* (《古今图书集成·七夕部》), during the reign of Emperor Gaozong of the Tang Dynasty:

> Royal lady Xu carved lotus roots and waternuts into the shape of queer birds and flowers, then presented them in crystal plates to His Majesty. So fascinated by the delicate artifacts, His Majesty lavished praises on Lady Xu and admired them all day long gleefully.

This tells us that the custom was observed in royal quarters from early times. Till today in Longnan and Tianshui of Gansu province, the pastries offered to Queen Qiao in Qiqiao celebrations at the beginning of July are still delicate and exquisite, showing superior craftsmanship.

In many areas of southern China, the event is related to Qiqiao in naming the gathering for pastry appraisal as "Qiao-tasting party" (吃巧). In some other areas, people make exquisite pastries as a ritualistic activity to honor the day, or gifts to give to their relatives, friends and neighbors to extend their good will.

According to an account in *An Extensive Collection of Literature of All Times* which was quoted from *The Annals of Jiangnan Area*, in Chongming county, "people eat pastries called Jiao'er (饺饵) on lunar July 7th as a tradition which is called 'tasting Qiao'". In Wujin county, "intellectuals and officials give delicate pastries as gifts to mark the day". According to *The Annals of Zhejiang*, in Wucheng

七夕文化透视 ▶▶▶
The Cowherd and the Weaver Fairy
A Study on the Folk Story and Double Seventh Day

county, "people give cakes made of eggplants and flour as gifts. In some cases, feasts are prepared to entertain friends and relatives as a break from the hot weather". In *The Annals of Jiangxi*, it is described as a common practice in Jianchang prefecture "for women to throw Qiqiao parties. They convene and pray under the moonlight offering as sacrifices fried pastries to Queen Qiao." In *The Annals of Fujian*, it is recorded that in Prefecture Zhangzhou, "girls conduct Qiqiao activities on the evening of lunar July 7th. They give off stir-fried beans as gifts to extend their good will."

In northern China, there is a tradition of giving pastries in a ritual known as "tasting Qiao". In northwestern provinces like Gansu and Shannxi, such pastries are sacrifices to be offered to Queen Qiao. In Xihe and Lixian counties of Gansu province, as Qiqiao celebrations last for many days, the sacrifices have to be replaced from time to time to maintain freshness. The pastries taken off the sacrificial table are shared among the married helpers as a reward for their work.

Another grand sacrificial ceremony called "Potluck Party" is conducted on the last day of Qiqiao celebration, another occasion for girls to showcase their cooking skills publicly apart from the pastry-making done for the sacrifices. It is also an important opportunity for younger girls to observe and learn.

Section 8　A Complete Cleaning-up of Cooking Utensils and Kitchen in General

Double Seventh Day, or the Qiqiao Festival as it is called in some places, has been regarded since ancient times as a festival dedicated to girls, or, more extensively, to women in general. In old China, women took on nearly all the household chores, including weaving, sewing and

cooking, which constituted a major part of their daily lives. Naturally, the Qiqiao Festival became a day when women would thoroughly clean their working environment and their working tools, particularly, the kitchen and cooking utensils. Apart from taste, the sanitary condition of the kitchen where meals were prepared became another standard to go by in deciding whether a housewife is skillful or not. In "The Festive Customs" from *An Extensive Collection of Literature of All Times*, a quotation from *The Annals of Zhili* reads as follows:

> On July 7th, girls thread needles under the moonlight, while housewives wash and clean oil containers and other kitchen potteries.

Why were oil containers particularly mentioned here? It's because they are greasy and used year-around. Once the old oil ran out, new oil would be poured into the containers right away for use. It was not uncommon for oil containers to remain greasy year-round, becoming contaminated on the outside by the mixture of oil drips, dust and smoke stains. Other kitchen potteries, too, were not washed daily after each meal like bowls, plates and cooking pots. Generally speaking, they were used for reservation of cooking materials which would last for a long time. It was both inconvenient and effort-consuming to clean them up frequently, thus they too were excluded intentionally or unintentionally from daily cleaning tasks. Cleaning kitchen on lunar July 7th reveals the importance people attached to hygienic conditions and food safety. The spirit of pursuing perfection and dexterity in whatever you do, just like what is expressed in other aspects of Qiqiao celebrations, is what we should value and enbrace even today.

七夕文化透视 ▶▶▶
The Cowherd and the Weaver Fairy
A Study on the Folk Story and Double Seventh Day

Section 9   Customs Concerning Embroidering and Weaving

In ancient times, embroidery was given great importance in the education of girls from well-to-do families, while weaving was the primary focus for girls from poor families. In "The Festive Customs" from *An Extensive Collection of Literature of All Times*, a quotation from *The Annals of Huguang* states:

> On the Double Seventh, women from poor families observe the day by weaving and spinning. There will be no Qiqiao parties. The intellectuals will get together and make a toast.

The Weaver Fairy, though in the folk story identified as the daughter of the Jade Emperor the supreme ruler of Heaven, was regarded by working-class people as "the other half", representing numerous ordinary peasant women who, along with their husbands, constituted the mainstay of Chinese feudal society. For thousands of years before the mid-20th century, almost 90% of the Chinese population lived in households where wives were responsible for weaving while husbands engaged in agricultural work. The Cowherd who represents male peasants, and the Weaver Fairy female peasants, got united in marriage out of their own wills. They worked hard to make a living and raise their kids. They tried hard for a good and happy life through their own labor. This was a common dream shared by all ordinary working people in ancient China. As prospective housewives who would take on most of household chores and family responsibilities, girls, on the day exclusively celebrated for them,

attach more importance to weaving and spinning.

In "An Introduction to Official Posts" in *The New Book of the Tang Dynasty* (《新唐书·百官志》), there is an account:

> The Bureau of Weaving and Dying conducts a sacrificial rite to honor looms on lunar July 7th.

The bureau responsible for weaving, dying and embroidery for royal court drafted the most outstanding weavers, dyers and embroiderers from all over the country. The offering of sacrifices to looms was actually a rite to worship the Weaver Fairy, or the Goddess of Weaving and Spinning. This account serves as a proof to the fact that lunar July 7th, as a folk festival, was so popular during the Tang Dynasty that relevant customs were already observed in official sacrificial ceremonies.

The popularity of the festival in Chinese society for so long is mostly out of people's approval of its theme which extols the marriage based on love and free will, the loyalty in marriage and the pursuit of happiness through hard work and frugality. While the festive celebrations have undergone adaptations and alterations throughout history for various reasons, core themes have remained relatively unchanged, as all kinds of competitions showcasing different skills and expertise can be traced back as to early as the Tang Dynasty.

By the way, we should be on alert against a recent trend in which some businessmen attempt to label the festival as "Chinese Lover's Day" in order to profit from the holiday economy. This is quite wrong. The word "lover" in Chinese usually implies "illegal or extramarital lovers", "a third party or mistress". We should not

七夕文化透视 ▸▸▸
The Cowherd and the Weaver Fairy
A Study on the Folk Story and Double Seventh Day

contaminate such a beautiful traditional festival which eulogizes loyalty in marriage with such a low, unethical label.

There is still much to learn and study about Double Seventh Day, or the Qiqiao Festival, but at the same time, we should not veer too off course, or lose our way. Trying to bring forth what's good and remain vigilant against what's bad should be a principle to go by in the momentum of promoting the cream of our traditional culture.

Chapter VI
Qiqiao Songs of Xihe County in History and Modern Times

As we have discussed earlier in this book, the age-old Qiqiao Festival celebrated in Xihe and Lixian counties of Gansu province is most probably a legacy of ancient Qin culture, and is closely related to ancient rites. My late father Zhao Zixian, a scholar and a enlightened gentleman from my hometown Xihe, collected and compiled local Qiqiao songs into a book in 1936. He thought highly of the Qiqiao Festival and Qiqiao songs, appreciating them for the realistic social implications, the rebellious spirit girls in feudal China showed against oppresive feudal ethics, the great concern for social reality and their eulogy of working life.

Held once a year, the Qiqiao Festival provides an important opportunity for girls to learn not only how to write verses for Qiqiao songs, sing and dance, but also how to improve their comprehensive expertise in life and work. The experiences accumulated and horizon broadened through participation in Qiqiao activities enable them to gain a better understanding of society, their fate, and life itself. In this sense, we can say that the Qiqiao Festival is an occasion where girls in feudal China engaged in self-teaching or hands-on education before entering marital life.

七夕文化透视 ▸▸▸
The Cowherd and the Weaver Fairy
A Study on the Folk Story and Double Seventh Day

Section 1   A Probe into the Qiqiao Customs after the Disruption of Feudal Ethics

Qiqiao customs practiced in Xihe and Lixian counties have a long history. In the past, Qiqiao activities among girls during the Qiqiao Festival were regarded as vulgar and unethical, thus were intentionally neglected by local intellectuals. During the Guangxu period of the Qing Dynasty, Ding Bingqian, the dean of Xihe Yangyuan Academy, wrote a poem describing the local grand Qiqiao celebrations, considering them a reminder of ancient rites. Once a former member of the Imperial Academy, Ding was a learned scholar influenced by reformist ideas in Beijing who disdained propagators of out-dated feudal conventions as well as the political opportunists who bent on seeking personal gains. He piled praises on the local Qiqiao activities, recognizing their progressive social implications in enlightening and educating girls.

Another scholar Zhao Yuanhe expressed similar opinion in his poem, only that he thought that the decisive factor for a person's deftness or smartness was "diligence" rather than blessings from immortals. Of course he was right and reasonable in his argument, but he ignored the role Qiqiao activities played in girls' socialization and cultivation of their free will. Due to remoteness of Xihe county, it remained disconnected from the fast-changing outside world. Therefore, many local intellectuals continued to base their judgements on Confucianism even in modern times. But at the same time, the remoteness and isolation make it possible for Xihe to keep Qiqiao customs in their original ancient form. Some Chinese experts on folklore studies regarded the Qiqiao customs in Xihe county as "having the longest history in China".

The study of Qiqiao customs and songs in Xihe county was initiated by my late father Zhao Zixian, who was then newly back home after he had completed studies in radio mechanics. Before that, he had enrolled himself in the First Army of the National Revolutionary Army under the command of general Feng Yuxiang and experienced the failure of the Northward Expedition. In both the poems he wrote in Tianjin in the 1930s, he touched upon the topic of Double Seventh Day celebration while expressing his love for his newly-wed wife. This probably explains why he organized his students to collect Qiqiao songs and compiled them into a book when he was back in Xihe, his hometown, in the summer of 1933 for the funeral of my grandma. He became a middle school teacher later, and was entrusted with running the local Institute for Mass Instruction by the local government. He also served at the same time as the head of the Association of New Life. He devoted himself to the enlightenment movements such as eliminating superstitions, fighting against mercenary marriage, encouraging women to oppose foot-binding, and publicizing the harm opium does on health. In 1935, he became a teacher at Gulou Nan Middle School. It was durig the following summer vacation that he started organizing his students to collect local Qiqiao songs, culminating in the compilation of a book titled *Xihe Qiqiao Songs* (《西河乞巧歌》).

The book *Xihe Qiqiao Songs* was compiled after the layout of *The Book of Songs*. The contents were divided into 3 categories: Ballads (feng, 风), Court Hymns (ya, 雅) and Eulogies (song, 颂). The songs reflecting marital reality and social customs go to the category "Ballads", while the ones about political rumors, legends and other stories are classified as "Court Hymns". The songs dedicated to the Qiqiao ritual or Queen Qiao on lunar July 7th are put under the category of "Eulogies". While many of his

七夕文化透视 ▶▶▶
The Cowherd and the Weaver Fairy
A Study on the Folk Story and Double Seventh Day

contemporaries considered these songs unethical and vulgar, not in line with Confucianism, my father's attempt to categorize them in a similar way to *The Book of Songs*, a Confucian classic, was undoubtedly bold and expressed his recognition on the value of those songs. Each category is further divided into several parts according to the content. For example, under the category "Ballads", there are three parts titled "Marital Life", "Ways and Customs" and "Working Skills". The Court Hymn category is further divided into two parts: "Political rumors" and "Legends and Stories", while the Eulogies are divided into four parts: "Welcoming of Queen Qiao", "Worshiping & Qiqiao", "Qiqiao with Bean Sprouts" and "Potluck Party and Seeing-off Rite". Qiqiao songs in Eulogies are mostly traditional ones which have been passed down from generation to generation.

To conclude the book, my father wrote two poems voicing his sympathy toward the girls in feudal society and his sharp criticism against the cruel oppression which had prevailed the whole society for so long. Taking the first poem as an example:

> The sad melodies are denouncement of us
> about girls suffering and bleeding of hearts.
> Sole plates folded and feet toes broken
> as tiny feet is a badge, or somewhat a token.
> Still it's not as hurting as an arranged marriage is to us
> where there's nothing we can do but curse.
> Praying for blessings from dear Queen Qiao,
> things will not get a little easier at all.
> Once a happy and cherished girl,
> how I miss my maiden life before!

In the Preface to *Xihe Qiqiao Songs*, there is a brief introduction to the history and circulation of Qiqiao songs as well as the geographical distribution of the Qiqiao custom practice in Xihe. It is stated like this:

The fact that Qiqiao customs in Xihe are mainly distributed along the Yang River and the Western Han River is thought-provoking. In "The Tribute of Yu" in *The Book of Documents* (*Shangshu*,《尚书·禹贡》), there is a sentence that reads: "The Yang River, which originates from mountain Bozhong flows eastward and becomes the Han River." This suggests that the Yang River is the source of the Western Han River. In ancient times, the Milky Way in the folk story of The Cowherd and the Weaver Fairy over which the couple meets on a magpie bridge once a year was called "Han" (numerous ancient literature pieces have proved this). This connection partly explains the significance of the Qiqiao Festival in Xihe county.

Du Fu, the most famous realistic poet in Chinese history, wrote a poem titled "The River of Heaven" (Tianhe,《天河》) when he came to Qinzhou prefecture in the year 759:

The Heavenly River[①]
Du Fu

Most of the time it may be hidden or fully visible,
but when autumn comes, it gets immediately bright.
Even if covered over by faint clouds,
in the long run it can be clear through the long night.
Full of stars, it stirs by paired palace gates,

---

① Translated by Stephen Owen, in *The Poetry of Du Fu* (《杜甫诗集》), published by De Gruyter in 2016.

七夕文化透视 ▸▸▸
The Cowherd and the Weaver Fairy
A Study on the Folk Story and Double Seventh Day

Moon's companion, it sinks by a frontier fort.

Oxherd and Weaver cross it every year,

and when have storms ever arisen thereon?

In the poem, the poet mentions that the moon is "clearest in autumn" and refers to the yearly reunion of the Cowherd and the Weaver Fairy. These details provide us with clues to the time background when the poem was written, most probably at the beginning of autumn. In the same collection of poetry, two lines from the subsequent poem titled "The New Moon" (《初月》) read like this, "Its light so thin, how could it be half-full?"[1] and "The Star River does not change its color"[2]. From this we can see that both the poems were written at the beginning of lunar July, that is, the beginning of autumn. The author pours his emotions and thoughts on the night onto the pages with his writing brush, allowing us a glimpse into the existence of this age-old story and the related customs in the area around Tianshui and Hanyuan (in ancient time under the jurisdiction of Qinzhou prefecture).

In the Preface, the author Mr. Zhao Zixian quotes numerous poems composed since the Tang Dynasty eulogizing Xihe as the source of the Han River along with those written about the Qixi Festival as well as related festive customs as the proof of the long history of this tradition. Thinking highly of the festival, he wrote:

---

[1] Translated by Stephen Owen, in *The Poetry of Du Fu*, published by De Gruyter Publishing House in 2016.

[2] Translated by Stephen Owen, in *The Poetry of Du Fu*, published by De Gruyter Publishing House in 2016.

Under the suffocating oppression of the feudal system and the bondage of rigid Confucian ideology, girls and young wives turned this festival into an occasion when their inner desires about life could be voiced. It is also a valuable and rare opportunity in feudal China to socialize with their peers. This is exactly where its value rests.

This is the first scientific and just assessment of the value of Qiqiao customs not only in Xihe, but also in Longnan, Tianshui, and even the whole country in general.

Section 2   What Is *Xihe Qiqiao Songs* about?

The Qiqiao songs collected in the book were mostly written before the 1930s, with the majority about miserable fate of women as well as their fight against oppressive feudal society. Critics on foot-binding, arranged-marriages, child-brides and other undesirable customs as well as out-dated social system are common themes in most of the songs. Some others touch upon various aspects of social life in Longnan, either on the life style, established customs in agricultural production, or rebellious movements against heavy taxes and levies, corruption, and incompetent officials who, scared of death, ran for their own lives when the whole city was at stake. Those songs record the pains and disasters inflicted on people by a divided regime, with local powers fighting each other for land and wealth, which stopped from no means to squeeze the people to their last blood. Compared with official documents of the time, the picture given in these songs is more reliable and convincing.

Some other songs in the book summarize the local ecological conditions, local specialties, life and working experiences as well

七夕文化透视 ▸▸▸
The Cowherd and the Weaver Fairy
A Study on the Folk Story and Double Seventh Day

as wisdom of life locals accumulated over generations. Girls were taught to learn about social life and the process of agricultural production through singing and chanting. Take "Twenty-four Solar Terms", the opening verse of the book, as an example:

> Bronze bell sounds from the top of a hill,
> when Start of Spring comes at January.
> White snow still caps the soaring hilltop,
> lest the rain water swash down like a mop.
> Waking of Insects comes with a thunder,
> turning awakened spiders into a busy hunter.
> When day and night are equally long,
> Spring Equinox persuades we to put spring clothes on.
> ...

The twenty-four solar terms are arranged in chronological order so as to teach girls ABCs of season shifts and climate changes. In Qiqiao songs, you will also find descriptions of various local products in Xihe.

The song titled "My nephew married off into a family near the southern Gate" introduced the handicraft industries in Xihe: the crowded blacksmiths' near the Eastern Gate, starch noodles made in Lujia Gou, firecrackers produced in Laozhuang village during the slack farming season, dried noodles made along the Ye's Road, bamboo-containers knitted in Wanjia Xia, grass-containers sold in Jiangjun Hill, and bamboo mats knitted in Shaijing Si, etc. All those are customized handicraft industries with established reputation for superior craftsmanship which has been passed down from generation to generation in each specific village or region.

Some Qiqiao songs extoll the skillful craftsmen and the

handicraft industries rich in local characteristics, showing the natives' pride in their hometown, just like what's expressed in the song "Dates on the Date Tree" which gives a detailed introduction to the local products of every town and village in Xihe. Still, other Qiqiao songs picture scenes of agricultural production such as in the song "Farming Around the Year" in which a vivid description of farmers' lives such as "digging wild roots to mix with wheat bran for our dinner" was given as a proof for farmers miserable lives in the old society.

In most parts of northwestern China, the Weaver Fairy embodies diligence and deftness. As she married to a peasant in defiance of the order from Queen Mother of the West, she set a shinning example for thousands of women fighting for freedom in love and against arranged marriages. During the Qiqiao celebrations, girls pray for blessings of wisdom and deftness from Queen Qiao through holding competitions showcasing different skills and expertise. "Qiao" in its connotation shows multi-layered aestheticism and perspectives of which Queen Qiao is the embodiment.

Girls eulogize Queen Qiao as a good-looking lady in the Qiqiao songs. They praise her hair, brows, eyes, nose and feet one by one in great detail, presenting a elegant fairy like from under an experienced brush. This is actually a painting of what they want to be in their imagination and a spur for self-improvement as they grow. Their prayers for blessings of skills in needlework including weaving, spinning, knitting, embroidering and tailoring as well as cooking express their earnest in commanding these working skills so as to lead a good life.

Before the 1940s, the remoteness of the Longnan district resulted in backwardness in education and a scarcity of schools. Girls in rural area were not granted access to education due to many reasons under feudal social system. Through the lines such as "Queen

Qiao, instruct me to read and write", girls' longing for knowledge and education is quite noticeable. In the Qiqiao songs, Queen Qiao is not only good at needlework and cooking, but also able to read and write, actually an expert in nearly every skills necessary in daily life. She was the idol of all girls in feudal China who aspired to a better life through hard work.

Some other songs condemning the pains opium inflicted on women and their families. There was no way out for them but to sell their sons and daughters, then kill themselves when nothing was left to be sold. In the song "All the Levies you have to pay General Kong", the cruel local military powers who resorted to every means to squeeze money out of the poor are sharply criticized, while in the songs "The Master Wang of Xihe" and "Brigade Commander Jiang has come to Xihe", good officials who helped and protected local people are praised.

We are also offered a glimpse into the important social events of that time through some of the songs. "Emperor Guangxu's flight to Xi'an" records the most sensational event happened in the late Qing Dynasty. "The Rebellion on July 15th" draws us a vivid picture of the local anti-tax rebellion at the end of the Qing Dynasty in which the rebellious peasants attacked the county sheriff and violently killed the county cleck. "The Seventh Day after the Winter Solstice" narrates the story of town dwellers voluntarily organizing themselves to fight against the gangster head Wang Youbang from Shaanxi. "The Earthquake before the Start of Autumn" refreshes the tragic memories of natural disaster, and so on. All those songs show girls' concern for local events and the security of their country.

搜集整理：赵逵夫

1 西庄和麻姐姐

Section 1　The Western Village and Sister Ramie

很早很早的时候，泾河①以北有一家人，夫妻两个都是庄稼汉，快三十岁了，生了一儿一女都没成②。找了个算命的问了一下，说是命属金，该往西才有后人，因为按五行说③，西方属金。这么着，两口子商量了一下就往西迁。

Long, long ago, there lived a couple to the north of Jing

---

① 泾河：黄河支流。发源于宁夏南部的六盘山东麓，向东南流经甘肃，在陕西高陵县入黄河最大支流渭河。

② 没成：方言，指夭夭。

③ 五行说：五行，我国古代称构成各种物质的五种元素，即水、火、木、金、土，见《尚书·甘誓》。认为五行相生：木生火、火生土、土生金、金生水；又相尅：水尅火、火尅金、金尅木、木尅土、土尅水。古代星相学家以相生相尅之理推算命运。又以五行和东、南、西、北、中相配，以金配西。

River[1]. Both approaching their 30s[2], the farmer and his wife were still expecting a child of their own, as their baby daughter and son had died young before. When they went to consult a fortune-teller about offspring, they were told to move west in order that their wish could be fulfilled, because West stands for Gold which they were in want of in their fate according to the theory of five elements[3]. Days later, the couple finally made up their minds to seek their fortune in the west.

　　他家里有一头大黄牛，驮了些东西，两口子又背了一些，走了一天，天黑了歇下来。第二天他说："再往西一些吧！"就又走。这么走了七天，到了汉水[4]边上，一个两河交叉的地方，全是没有开的闲地。两口子商量说："都说'泾河短，汉水长，

---

① 　Jing River: one of the branches of the Yellow River which originates on the east slope of Liupanshan Mountain in Ningxia Hui Autonomous Region and runs southeast through Gansu province to join the Wei River, the largest branch of the Yellow River, in Shaanxi province.

② 　Ancient Chinese got married young, with men at around 17 and women around 15. As they attached great importance to the continuation of family bloodline, mostly they would have their first baby before their 20s.

③ 　The theory of Five Elements: According to ancient Chinese wisdom, the five elements which make up every matter in this world are water, fire, wood, gold and earth. These five elements can generate each other, such as the generation of fire by water, earth by fire, gold by earth and water by gold. So they can overpower each other too, such as the overwhelming of fire by water, gold by fire, wood by gold, earth by wood and water by earth. The ancient Chinese astrologist practiced fortune-telling or sooth-saying by referring to the theory of five elements. The five directions in space, that is, the east, the south, the west, the north and the middle were matched with the five elements, too. Thus, gold was matched with West.

④ 　汉水：公元前，今西汉水在略阳一直向东，沔水为其重要支流，统称为"汉水"。后由于地震原因其上游在略阳以西淤塞而折向南流，入嘉陵江，才分为西汉水、东汉水（沔水）两条河流。

一年能打两年粮。'就在这里安家吧！"

They loaded most of their belongings on the back of their cow and carried the rest on their backs, embarking on their westward journey. West and west they went, until it was dusk, then they stopped for the night. The following morning, they decided to move west further to make sure it was far enough. Seven days had passed before they finally decided to settle down. In front of them, a wild expanse of uncultivated land stretched out at the confluence of two branches of the Han River[①]. "As the old saying goes: 'The Jing River is short and the Han River is long, people living along them are happy and strong'. The land here must be fertile. Let's make our home here." The couple talked it over and happily decided to have their new house built there.

那时正是春季，他们挖了一眼窑，开了一些地，种上了庄稼。第二年，真的生了一个儿子。因为按算命先生说命里属金，迁到西面才成了的，就取名叫"金成"。过了几年，又先后迁来些人家，听了先迁来这家人的事，也就把这个庄叫"西庄"。

It was spring. They dug out a cave house, cultivated tracts of wasteland and planted crops in it. Sure enough in the following year, the wife gave birth to a baby boy whom they named as Jincheng ("Blessed with gold element"). As years went by, small throngs of people came and gathered around their house, gradually developing

---

① The Han River: Before the Common Era, the West Han River headed east from Lueyang county in what is now Shaanxi province, with the Mian River as its main branch. Later, the upper reaches of the West Han River bent to head south from the west of Lueyang county as a result of an earthquake and finally joined the Jialing River. From then on, the former Han River split into two—the West Han River and the East Han River (the Mian River).

the place into a village which they named as West Village to honor the couple—the first settlers here and their life story.

后面来的人当中，有一个女子，从小给人当童养媳，什么苦活都干，只为没生养，被公公家不要了，赶回娘家。别的人家一听不生养，也没有来说亲的。她爹娘也都因为这事心上吃了亏，病死了。她爹娘死后，哥哥、嫂子嫌她住家里房、吃家里饭，常常指桑骂槐冷待她，她受不了就从家里跑出来了。

Among the villagers, there was a young woman who had been married off very young to a family as a child bride[1]. Toiled day and night but still abused by her parents-in-law, she was finally thrown out of her husband's on the excuse that she failed to give birth to a baby[2], which denied her another chance of getting married. Sorrow-stricken, her parents died soon, leaving her despised by her elder brother and the sister-in-law. They hated to support her, treated her terribly and bullied her with bitter tongue. When she couldn't stand it any longer, she ran away from her brother's.

---

[1] Child bride: Before the liberation of China in 1949, poor families which were unable to support their kids would give away or sell their daughters at a very young age to the families with sons as child brides. They were actually unpaid child labors for the families which took them in. Though most of these girls toiled all day long, they were terribly abused by their in-laws and died young of malnutrition or abuse. If some of them did grow up, they would marry a son from the family. That's why they were called child bride.

[2] Offspring was of vital importance to the ancient Chinese. The failure to bring a child, especially a boy, a justified heir to a family was regarded a grave sin for a wife. According to ancient Chinese belief, among seven grounds to dismiss a wife, bearing no child topped the list, even ranked before adultery and impiety.

金成爹、金成娘听着她可怜，就收留下来。这女子有一个本事，是捻麻线、织麻布、缝麻布衫、做麻鞋，都做得又快又好。她让金成爹按她说的做了一个纺麻线的纺车，用脚踏着带动几根线杆子转，只要一面踩踏板，一面调理麻叶，纺的线又细又匀，一个人顶几个人。后来又做了一个织布机，织的麻布又薄又光。金成娘让金成叫她"麻姐姐"，庄里人也都称她为"麻姐姐"。

Having pity on her, Jincheng's parents took her in like a family. The woman was gifted in work such as spinning ramie yarn, weaving ramie cloth, sewing ramie clothes and making ramie shoes. She could get all these work done quickly and well. Then, she asked Jincheng's father to make a spinning wheel after her drawing draft. When it was done, she only needed to tread on a pedal connected to spinning poles and adjust the ramie leaves to get thin and sleek ramie yarns. This machine improved her spinning efficiency tremendously. She again asked Jincheng's father to make her a loom, which produced thin and soft ramie cloth, too. Because of her superior skills in making ramie products, Jincheng affectionately called her "Sister Ramie", which was then taken on by other villagers as a nickname.

因为那时候人冬天都是穿羊皮、牛皮啥的缝的衣裳，夏天穿麻织的衣裳，富贵人家、大官才穿绸子做的。这么着，庄里一些女孩子、媳妇子都向麻姐姐学手艺，照麻姐姐的纺车自己也请木匠作纺车，照麻姐姐的织布机自己也请木匠做织布机。

At that time, winter attire were primarily made of sheepskin or cowhide, while ramie fabric was the preferred choice for summer clothing. Only the really rich and powerful wore silk during the summer. Therefore, ramie spinning and weaving were very important skills for housewives and would-be housewives in ordinary families, as they were the ones who are responsible for the year-round clothing of the whole family. Sister Ramie generously passed on her skills to village girls, housewives, introducing them to the spinning wheel and loom through her teachings.

※

这家也请，那家也请，麻姐姐没有分身术，有时就说："你先去，我后面来。"请的人说："你知道我家吗？"麻姐姐说："能寻着。"由此，现在人们跳麻姐姐① 时还唱："麻姐姐，魂来了，黑天半夜寻来了。"

She was wanted by so many girls and housewives for home instruction that sometimes when she was occupied in one house and could not spare time for another, she would politely ask the person who had come to see her: "Would you go back first? I will join you soon." The visitor would ask: "All right. But do you know the way to my house?" "Surely I do." Sister Ramie would answer. That's why even today during Qiqiao celebration, when the Sister Ramie dance is performed[2], the girls would sing: "Sister Ramie is on her way, she will join you without delay."

※

这麻姐姐呢，一来年龄越来越大了，二来看到很多公公婆婆糟践媳妇子，弄得媳妇子左也不是，右也不是，一天忙得要

---

① 乞巧仪式的一部分，唱赞颂和邀请麻姐姐降临的歌。
② Part of the Skill-begging rites in which girls and young women express their admiration of Sister Ramie as well as Queen of Dexterity through singing and dancing.

死，还三天两头挨打；有的男人帮媳妇子解释一下，婆婆就说儿子"没刚性，啥都听媳妇儿的"。麻姐姐就想，还不如一个人过，自己做活自己吃，谁的气也不受。金成爹后来在离自家土窑不远处也给她挖了一眼窑，两家也常互相帮忙，和一家人一样。

As years went by, Sister Ramie gradually gave up hope for remarrying. She had witnessed so many daughters-in-law being enslaved and abused by their parents-in-law all year round without any hope of escaping from the misery. Even occasional defense on the wives from their husbands would be scolded by their in-laws as "being henpecked" and "lacking a husband's authority", leading to even more severe harms. Upon witnessing such unjustices, Sister Ramie decided to live on her own, as she believed that she could support herself through hard work without taking bullies from anybody. On this decision of hers, Jincheng's father said nothing, but dug out another cave-house near their own for her. Living close by, the two families got along well and treated each other like a family.

2 牛郎和神牛

Section 2   Cowherd and the Magical Ox

金成长到十岁的时候，他娘又生了一个儿子，这就是牛郎。

牛郎生下来一百天的时候，麻姐姐和庄里一些邻居来给这月娃子过"百岁"[①]。麻姐姐说："叫这娃也来个抓岁[②]，看将来是

---

① 陇南一带在小孩一百天时有"过百岁"的风俗。

② "抓岁"即"抓周"。

七夕文化透视 ▸▸▸
The Cowherd and the Weaver Fairy
A Study on the Folk Story and Double Seventh Day

个干啥的。"家里就在炕上摆了些铲子、铁勺、织布梭、牛铃铛啥的，又借了木匠的尺子、石匠的锤子，还有笔和秤，摆了一大圈。可这娃一手抓着了大铃铛，摇了两下。

When Jincheng was ten years old, his mother gave birth to another boy who was later named as Jinling (means in Chinese "golden bell" and who grew up to be the Cowherd). When the baby was one-hundred-day old, Sister Ramie and some other villagers came to celebrate his "one-hundred-day birthday"[①]. Sister Ramie suggested: "Let's conduct a 'lot-drawing' ritual for the baby to see what he would be when he grows up." They then put various objects such as a scoop, a shuttle, a cowbell, a carpenter's ruler, a stonemason's hammer, a writing brush and a rod scale on a table for the baby to grab. Held in his mother's arms, the baby immediately picked up the cowbell and shook it several times.

金成他爹说："看来这儿子和他哥一样，是跟上我打牛后半截子的。"大家问叫啥名子，他爹说："还没取，就叫金铃算了。他哥叫金成，他叫金铃。"大家都说："金铃精灵，这娃精灵着呢！"这么着，这娃名子就叫了"金铃"。

Jincheng's father exclaimed: "It's likely that we will have another cowherd, just like me and his elder brother!" When asked about the boy's name, the father replied: "He hasn't been named yet. Since he chose the cowbell, let's just call him Jinling." At this, the guests applauded, saying: "What a good name! 'Jinling' sounds just like "smart" (in Chinese). To be sure, the boy will be smart and

---

① The locals of the Longnan area in Gansu province traditionally celebrate the first hundred days that a baby survives, as the mortality rate was quite high in the old days. Relatives, friends and neighbors are invited to a feast to share the family's happiness.

resourceful!" Hence, the boy got his name.

就在金铃生下来两天的时候，他家那头老黄牛也生了一个牛娃儿。那老牛刚刚把它身上给舔干，这牛娃儿就站起来，没有去咂奶子，却走到那窑门口朝炕上叫。那月娃子，就是那金铃也叫了起来。他爹、他娘都说："这牛娃儿就好像和这娃有啥缘分呢。脚跟脚一起来到世上，还这么着打招呼呢！"

Two days after Jinling's birth, the family's old cow gave birth to a calf. The moment the calf struggled out of its mother's body and was barely licked dry, it managed to stand up unsteadily. Instead of approaching its mother for milk, the calf toddled to the door of the cave-house and mooed towards *kang*[1] where Jinling was, to which Jinling responded with babbling. The father and mother exclaimed: "There seems to be some predestined connection between the boy and the calf—they came to this world nearly at the same time and are so eager to greet each other!"

原来这牛是天上的金牛星，因为犯了天条被贬下凡间消罪，玉帝让太白金星领他下凡投胎。太白金星给金牛星说："汉水和天相通，你投到汉水边，万一玉帝忘记，你回来诉说也多一条路。"又说："汉水上游只有一家的牛是泾河边上来的早胜牛[2]，体大身高，好怀得下你，你就投他家。"这么的金牛星就投在了金成家。

The calf was actually the Golden Ox Star[3] which had been

---

①   *Kang*: a heatable brick bed common in northern China.

②   甘肃省庆阳市宁县南部有一地名"早胜"，位于泾河以上、马莲河东侧。当地有一种牛个头高大，毛色鲜亮，当地叫早胜牛。

③   For ancient Chinese, each of the 28 constellations in the sky stands for a god, among which there was a Ox Star, thus a god "Golden Ox Star".

banished from the Heavenly Court for misdeeds. The punishment was to be reborn as an ox. As the Jade Emperor[1] ordered Great White Venus[2] to guide it to its reincarnation, the latter then proposed to the Golden Ox: "The Han River is connected with the Heavenly Court through the Milky Way, so we'd better put you there—in case the Jade Emperor forgets about you when your term is over, you may come up along the river and appeal before the Emperor in person." He then added: "For your size and build, there is only one Zaosheng cow[3] from the Jing River in the upper reaches of the Han River which is strong and big enough to carry you in her belly." So the Golden Ox was born here as a little calf.

说来也奇怪，这金铃一两岁的时候，大人拔草，把他放在地边上，他也寻着拔草，不拔番麦[4]苗；大人晒了粮食，他一看见鸟儿就叫喊，走过去赶；有洒在地上的麦颗儿，他一颗一颗捡起来，拿给他娘。有时洒的粮食多，他就一直蹲着捡，大半天动都不动。

Jinling showed his uncommonness at the age of one or two. To the elders' amazement, when he helped with pulling out weeds

---

[1] The Jade Emperor, the imagined supreme deity in Taoism, the Ruler of the Heavenly Court where the gods live.

[2] The Great White Venus: Among the 28 constellations, Venus was an important star, thus the god incarnated as Venus tops the gods' list in the Heavenly Court.

[3] Zaosheng cow: "Zaosheng" is a place in the south of Ning county in the present day Qingyang city, Gansu province. It is located by the upper reach of the Jing River and east to the Malian River. The place is noted for an excellent breed of cow named after it, which is famous for its tall and stout build as well as bright-colored bristles.

[4] 番麦：玉米。

in the cornfield, he never mixed the corn seedlings with the weeds. He would shoo off, sometimes toddled over to drive away the birds which were pecking at grains for sun-drying. He would pick up grains left on the ground one by one and gave them to his mother. Sometimes, he squatted picking up grains from the ground without moving for a couple of hours in a row.

金铃四五岁的时候，他哥帮着他爹、他娘在地里干活，他就放牛，后来又带上割草。地里忙的时候，他也送饭，又帮着锄地、背粪、撒粪、点籽。

At the age of four or five, when his brother had joined their parents in field work, Jinling started herding the cattle. Later on, he would cut grasses for the cows at the same time. During the busy farming season, he would bring meals to the field for his family, carry manure to and from the field for fertilizer, or plough and plant along with his family.

过了几年，有一天，金成爹说："金铃长大了，家里多了一双手，可金成也大了。男大当婚，女大当嫁，又得给大儿子说妇人了。"金成娘说："全家子一眼窑，一个炕，咋娶媳妇子哩？"第二天，金成爹开始给大儿子打窑。

Several years later, Jincheng's father talked it over with his wife: "Jinling is a big help now, and Jincheng is old enough to get married. It's high time we found him a good wife." Jincheng's mother sighed: "Yes, you are quite right. But we have only one cave-house and one kang for the whole family. How can we persuade any girl to marry into such a poor family?" Upon hearing this, Jingcheng's father fell silent, but got up early the next morning to dig another cave-house as the bridal chamber for his elder son.

那打窑可不像挖地，不是向下使劲，常常要朝着头顶上挖。踩在板凳上，抬起镢头朝顶上一点一点往下削。不好出劲不说，土还往眼睛里掉。如碰到有一块大石头在顶上，那可就难收拾了。因为岁数也大了，一眼窑打成，金成爹腰疼、背疼，一辈子苦下的病全都来了，吃了几服药也不见好，便过世了。

Cave-digging is much tougher work than farming. Most of the time, he had to stand on a chair digging strenuously upward or sideways, with bits of earth kept flying into his eyes. His neck and shoulders hurt badly due to the long hours of labor. But all those were nothing compared with a piece of unexpected big rock protruding from the ceiling during the process, which would be very dangerous and effort-consuming to get rid of. Already advanced in years, when the cave-house was finally done, Jincheng's father was down with illness and exhaustion. Medicine was used in vain. The father died before long.

金成他爹的三年①过了以后，金成就成了亲。金成她娘想，不管咋着，把老汉②死的时候惦记的事办成了，自己也了了一层心事。可没多长时间她就看出来，这媳妇子心眼多，有啥好东西，只往他两口子的窑里藏，有啥事不叫男人和娘商量，动不动就说："大儿子不当家，谁当家！"

---

① 三年：指父母去世儿女守孝三年。
② 老汉：常指年老的男子，方言中指自己的丈夫。

Three years later, after the mourning[1] period for his father had ended, Jincheng got married. Jincheng's mother was relieved to have her husband's last wish fulfilled. However, it did not take long for her to realize that her daughter-in-law was a tricky and calculating woman who habitually sneaked goodies into their own cave-house and put others' needs out of her consideration at all. The woman also urged her husband to make decisions regarding family affairs without consulting his mother, saying: "The eldest son was born to be the head of the family! Who could say no to this?"

金成成家以后，麻姐姐还是和以前一样经常来他家走动。每次来都会教金成媳妇子捻麻线、织麻布，也常拿些萝卜、黄瓜什么的。

Sister Ramie paid regular visits to Jincheng's just like before. On every visit, she either brought vegetables she had planted herself or tutored Jincheng's wife in spinning and weaving.

有时金成娘想留她吃饭，金成媳妇子就说："麻姐姐，听说你住的那窑还是死了的我爹给你打的？"麻姐姐说："就是的。"金成媳妇子就说："那我爹沾上你的啥光了呀？"麻姐姐一听，也就不再在金成家吃饭。可她心里还是感激金成爹、金成娘，

---

[1] In the past, there was a custom of observing a three-year mourning period for one's deceased parents. This custom can be traced back to the Zhou Dynasty. During those three years, sons and daughters either lived in a shack beside their parent's tomb, or stayed at home mourning. Bright-colored dresses and ornaments were considered inappropriate, with feasts and other joyful entertainments completely forbidden. Weddings and celebrations would be avoided and those holding an official post usually resigned from their positions to stay home and mourn.

对金成媳妇子也还是好好的，有啥要教的都实心实意地教。金成娘操心劳累，又遇上这样的儿媳妇，心上不畅快，没有多久也过世了。金成娘过世以后，麻姐姐除了金成媳妇子来叫帮着收拾纺车什么的，就不太到金成家去。

Sometimes when Jincheng's mother invited Sister Ramie to stay for dinner, Jincheng's wife would ask: "Sister Ramie, is it true that the cave-house you are staying in now was dug by my father-in-law?" Sister Ramie would answer: "Yes, it is." The wife would ask again: "Then what did my father-in-law get in reward?" Sister Ramie then realized how her goodwill had been taken for granted by Jincheng's wife. Although thankful for what Jincheng's parents had done for her, she decided to distance herself from the family thereafter. Weakened by lifelong toil and upset with her daught-in-law, Jincheng's mother passed away, too. After the old woman's death, Sister Ramie continued to help Jincheng's wife with her spinning and weaving, but paid visits to Jincheng's only on request.

金铃自从娘死了以后，除了吃饭、睡觉，地里有活地里干，地里没活就赶了牛到坡上去。那一头老黄牛在金成娘死后时间不长也死了。家里有些事，他给他哥不好说，怕骂仗①，只好忍着。有些话给麻姐姐也不好说。与他最亲密，又什么话都可以说的，就只有那头从生下来就对他特别亲的黄牛。

Since his mother's death, Jinling took over almost all the field work. He would work all day long in the field during the busy farming season or herd cows on the mountain slope, intentionally avoided staying at home except for eating or sleeping. Soon after his mother's death, the old cow died, too. To avoid fights and

---

① 骂仗：吵架。

quarrels, Jinling swallowed abuses from his sister-in-law quietly. He chose to hold those unpleasant household trifles from Sister Ramie as well. His only faithful listener who accompanied him through those hard times was the calf, his closest pal ever since they were born.

金铃在外放牛时，要看到庄里的烟冒起来后再等一锅水烧开的时间，才会回家。有时牛吃饱了卧着，金铃割够了给牛的柴草，捆好放着，就爬在牛旁边给牛说话。那牛也给他"哞——！哞——！"地叫着，有时给他点头，有时给他摇头。他觉得牛能听懂他的话。牛点头的事，他就做；牛摇头的事，他就不做。

At dusk, Jinling would wait till the smoke from chimneys had curled and swayed in sky for long enough to boil a pot of water before he went back home. Sometimes, when all the work was done—with the ox full and satisfied, firewoods and grasses for cows cut and tied up into a neat roll—Jinling would lie on his belly and confide his sorrows and happiness to the ox who mooed to him while nodding or shaking its head now and then as if in response. Jinling believed that the ox understood him and was telling him what he should do or not, which he followed readily.

有一次天还早，牛就朝回家的路上走，拉也拉不住。刚回家，大白雨①就来了，像勺泼的一样，沟里的水比河还大。从那以后金铃就把牛信到骨头里去了。

One day, when it was still early, the ox pulled him stubbornly

———————
① 白雨：暴雨。

in the home direction and refused to give up no matter how hard he pulled its reins otherwise. Helplessly, Jinling followed it home. No sooner had they got back home than a heavy downpour thrashed down with ditches and gullies soon overflowed. From then on, Jinling had no more doubts about the ox's wisdom.

�֎

有一次，麻姐姐看见金铃摘了些漆颠儿①吃，才知道金铃放完牛背了草回家，常常灶边上只给他留了一点清汤，金铃肚子饿吃不饱就常摘漆颠儿、野果子啥的填肚子。她就把金铃叫到自己家，给些吃的。后头她也常常避开人，叫金铃到她家吃一点，有时看见金铃赶了牛要上坡去，没有人时，赶紧塞给一块馍，让金铃揣在怀里，带到坡上去吃。

One day, Sister Ramie spotted Jinling eating sprouts from a lacquer tree. When asked, Jinling confided to her that most of the times he returned home after a day's work herding cows and cutting grasses in the field and the woods, he could only find a bowl of thin soup on the edge of cooking stove for dinner. Going hungry most of the time, he could only look for food such as edible sprouts of plants or wild berries in the woods or among the bushes to fill his empty stomach. On hearing this, Sister Ramie took Jinling to her cave and fed him. It was then developed into a secret routine. From time to time when nobody was looking, she would slip a piece of steamed bun into the boy's hand on his way to field work. The boy and Sister Ramie became even closer to each other when years went by.

---

① 漆颠儿：漆树上的嫩芽，样子像香椿。一般在大林里有。

3 牛郎分家

Section 3 The Split-up

有一天，金铃割了一大捆蒿柴，看天还早，就躺在坡上，可那牛直向家里走。他也就背了柴跟着回家。一到家，看到他哥、他嫂子包了肉饺子吃。他哥说："你嫂子给你留下着哩。"他嫂子气呼呼地把自己碗里的拨了几个给他。他吃着确实香得很，长这么大还没吃过这么香的肉饺子。

One day, when Jinling had got a big bundle of firewood cut, it was still early, so he lay down on the mountain slope to take a nap. But before he dozed off, to his great surprise, the ox turned to head home directly, so he got up hastily, picked up the bundle and followed on its heels. On entering the cave-house, he caught sight of his brother and sister-in-law by the dining table eating dumplings. His brother greeted him and said: "Your sister-in-law had put some aside for you. Come and eat." Upon which the woman angrily poked several out of her bowl into his. Dumplings made of minced meat tasted so good that he believed he had never had anything as yummy.

第二天放牛，他把柴草割了一大捆放下，看时间还早就靠着柴草睡着了。他睡得懵里懵懂的，听见牛给他说话："今天你哥送你嫂子回娘家去了，桌子上放着半碗饺子，灶台上放着一块饼子。那饼子你千万不要吃，里面有毒！"他一听这话就惊醒了，看到那牛正盯着他。他问："是你给我说话吗？"那牛点了点头。他又问："那你怎么知道的？"问了半天，那牛只是对

七夕文化透视 ▸▸▸
The Cowherd and the Weaver Fairy
A Study on the Folk Story and Double Seventh Day

着天空叫："哞——！哞——！"金铃也就不问了。

The following day, when he again was done cutting firewood and it was still early, he cuddled against the firewood bundle for a nap. In a dreamlike trance, he heard the ox talked to him: "Your elder brother and his wife were away to your sister-in-law's today. You may find half a bowl of dumplings on the dining table and a piece of pancake on the kitchen table. The pancake is poisonous. Don't touch it!" At this Jinling woke up with a start to find the ox gazing at him attentively. Jinling asked: "Was it you who talked to me just now?" The ox nodded. Jinling asked again: "How did you know that?" At that the ox mooed into the sky in response, so he left it at that.

他晚上回去，哥哥、嫂子真的都不在，桌上放着半碗饺子，灶台上放着一块饼子。他拿起那块饼子看了一下，心想："我把这给狗吃了，看黄牛说的是不是真的。"就把饼子拿出来扔给看大门的狗。那狗看是一块饼子，两口吃了，吃完了就一下躺在地上，四条腿乱蹬、乱叫，没多大时间就断气了。

When he got back home, sure enough, there was not a soul in, only half a bowl of dumplings on the dining table and a piece of pancake on the kitchen table. He picked up the pancake and murmured to himself: "Let's see if it's true." So he fed the watchdog in the courtyard with the pancake. No sooner had the dog swallowed down the pancake in several bites than it slumped onto the ground whining, its limbs twitching. In no time it breathed its last breath and died.

金铃就只把饺子吃了，又吃了点萝卜啥的，睡了。半夜金铃去给牛添草的时候，摸着牛的头说："黄牛，真是多亏了你，

没有你我早就没命了！"那牛抬起头来把他看了好大一会儿，说："你哥、你嫂子要和你分家了！"金铃一听牛真的对他说话了，高兴地把脸靠在牛的脸上亲热了一下说："只要有你，我啥都不怕！"牛说："你只要我就成了，别的啥都不要。"金铃说："我记下了！"

Jinling ate the dumplings plus some radishes before he went to bed. At mid-night, when he got up to add mid-night fodder for the ox, he patted it on its head affectionately and said: "My old pal, I owe you my life. I would have been a dead man if it's not for you." The ox raised its head, gazed at him for a while, and said: "Your elder brother and sister-in-law are thinking of dividing the family property with you." Joyful to hear it speaking, Jinling rubbed his face on its forehead and murmured: "I'm afraid of nothing as long as I'm with you!" The ox then told him: "Take me only at the property-division." Jinling nodded.

第二天，他哥回来看见自家看门的狗躺在院里死了，就问金铃，金铃如实说了。他哥不信。过了两天他嫂子回来，他哥问怎么灶台上放的饼子里有毒，把狗都毒死了。他嫂子说："那是我放下的毒老鼠的，金铃拿着去把狗毒死了，又给你说是我要毒他。我看他不把这个家整散不开心！"说着要去打金铃，他哥硬拉住，她就瘫到地上打滚，又哭又闹，一口一个"要分家"，又说："这屋里有我没他，有他没我！"

The following day, when Jincheng got back, he found the watchdog lying dead and stiff in the courtyard. When asked, Jinling told his brother everything, but his brother refused to believe what he had said. Two days later, when his sister-in-law came back, his brother questioned her about the poisonous pancake. The woman cried and screamed: "I left the poisonous pancake there for mice, but your brother poisoned the watchdog instead. Now he wronged me for trying to murder him! How mischievous! Is he thinking of tearing apart the family?" With this she dashed forward to hit Jinling. When her husband held her back, she threw herself onto the ground kicking and thrashing around, yelling repeatedly: "Divide the family property right away! Immediately! I cannot share a roof with your brother any longer!"

他哥叫妇人闹得没办法，怕邻居笑话，就对金铃说："兄弟，你看这么下去也不是个样子，再说在一个锅里搅，你不放心，我也不放心。我看分就分了吧！"

Nonplussed and ashamed, his brother pleaded with Jinling: "Dear brother, it seems there is nothing I can do about it now. To scoop food out of one pot is no longer a good idea for both of us. Let's divide the family property then." To which Jinling agreed.

他们就请了庄里岁数大一些，也识几个字的两个老汉来主持分家。那两个老汉把家里的地有多少、粮食有多少，都问了一下，就要一样一样来分，那金铃可抢着说："别的我都不要，只要那一头牛。"那两个老汉说："先分地，地分了别的家当再总分成两份，你弟兄两个挑。"金铃说："两位大爸也不要麻烦了，我地也不要，粮也不要，别的家当也不要，只要那头牛。"

They then invited two literate respectable elders of the village to preside over family property-division. After having totaled the family property such as the acreage of farmland and the amount of grain reserve, the elders were about to divide them evenly between the two brothers when Jinling cut in: "No need for trouble, dear uncles. I want nothing except the ox."

　　这两个老汉看金铃没了娘和老子常受嫂子的气，还有点想偏心他，看他这么犟也没办法。他嫂子走过来问："那口窑也不要？"金铃说："不要。"他嫂子赶紧说："两位大爸要在文书上写明白，不能反悔！"

The elders who took pity on Jinling because of what he had suffered since his parents' death were greatly surprised. They had intended to help him in the division and were quite unprepared to hear that. His sister-in-law rushed over hastily and asked: "You do not want even the cave-house?" "No." Jinling answered. His sister-in-law then urged the two elders: "Dear uncles, please write it down in black and white right now in case somebody goes back on his words!"

　　那两位老汉来时也带着纸呀、笔砚呀啥的，就写了"金铃自愿只要黄牛一头"。最后叫弟兄两个按了手印。那写分家文书的老汉对金铃说："前头你是个放牛的牛郎，从今儿你就真成了两袖清风的牛郎了！"后来庄里人一提起金铃来，也就都叫他"牛郎"。

With writing brush and ink ready, the elders had to write down on the paper: "Jinling voluntarily gives up everything except the ox." on which the two brothers put their thumb prints. The elders sighed, turned and talked to Jinling: "In the past you herded the cow all day long. Now you've become a real penniless cowherd." And this was how Jinling got his nickname "Cowherd".

4 牛郎织女成夫妻

Section 4　The Cowherd and the Weaver Fairy
Became Husband and Wife

牛郎和他哥哥分家只要了一头牛。分完家跑到牛圈里给牛说了分家的结果，黄牛点了点头，说："我领你去一个地方。"牛郎就牵了牛出来，他哥给装了些面、粮食叫他带上，说："你这几天总得吃呀！"他嫂子在窑里隔着窗子喊："白纸黑字写的分给我家的，白白送人！"金铃想不拿，但看到哥哥一定要给，怕伤了哥哥的心，就驮在牛身上。

The ox was the only property Cowherd got from the family property-division. He told the ox the result and the latter nodded: "Follow me. We will go somewhere." So Cowherd pulled its reins and was about to leave when his brother thrust several grain bags into his arms and said: "No matter what, you have to get something to eat before settling down." At that his sister-in-law yelled from behind the window: "Why throwing away our grain like this? It is ours now and everything had been written down in black and white at property-division!" Ignoring what she had said, his brother insisted that he took it. Unwilling to break his brother's heart, Cowherd took the grain bags and put them on the back of the ox before they left the house.

出了院，金铃只是跟着黄牛走。走到河边，一人一牛饮了点水，就顺着一条河向南走。走了大半天，到了一个地方，一

面是山，一面是水，一大片草坡没有人耕种过，牛立下不走了。牛郎向四面一看，说："真是个好地方啊！"那牛也连连点头。

Once out on the road, the ox took the lead and Jinling followed it. They stopped by a river and drank some water, then headed all the way southward. They went and went till the river led them to an expanse of uncultivated land at the foot of a mountain where the ox stopped. Looking around, Cowherd exclaimed: "Oh my! What a good tract of land!" To that the ox nodded in agreement.

牛郎就找了一个高一点、平一点的地方，把粮食、面啥的先卸下来，放开牛去吃草。他想砍几棵树搭一个草棚，可没斧头。他看见牛在喝水，自己也渴了，就去河边喝水，猛然看到河边上有一把斧头。牛郎说："这是谁遗下的？先借上用一下。"就砍了四棵小树，拔了一些蒿草，搭了一个草棚，里头铺了一些干草，躺了下来。

Cowherd then unloaded the grain bags onto a raised flat terrace on the mountain slope and let go of the ox for grazing. He planned to build a shed with tree branches and hay, but there was no ax. Sulkily, he went to the river and joined the ox in drinking. But there on the ground by the river laid an ax! Joyfully, Cowherd picked it up and murmured to himself: "Whose ax is this? Maybe I can borrow it for a moment." Afterwards, he hacked down four trees and pulled some dry grass stalks to make a shed. When it was done, he paved the ground with hay and lay down for a rest.

躺了一会儿，牛郎心想：该做饭了，没有锅、碗、勺咋办？出了棚子，走了几步，看见一个土坎坎儿下有一个锅、一把切刀、一把圆凿子。牛郎高兴地说："太好了！这不是打猎的遗下的，就是砍树的遗下的，先借上用。用斧头和这切刀、圆凿子就能做个木勺、木碗，还可以做树皮的筒筒装面啥的。"他先把饭做着吃了，把牛也拉在草棚里一起睡。

A while later, Cowherd thought: "It's time for dinner, but there was no pot, no bowl, no scoop, nothing. What can I do?" Helplessly, he went out of the shed and looked around. To his great joy, he found a pot, a cutting knife and a chisel under a hanging earthen edge nearby. Cowherd laughed happily: "How lucky I am! Whose utensil are these? The hunter's? The logger's? No matter to whom they belong, I have to borrow them now. I can use the ax and the cutting knife to make wooden bowls and scoops as well as a bark barrel for flour." He then had dinner and retired into the shed with the ox for the night.

第二天天不亮牛郎就起来，想："庄稼人有了地就有了活命。"要挖地，可没镢头咋做呢？牛郎正在犯愁，走出草棚不远看见一把镢头。他不管三七二十一，先提起来挖。一直挖到天黑，也不嫌乏。第三天他又天不亮起来，想："这地方也平，土也软，应该做一个杠头①，我和老牛一起耕，那才快！"提了斧头就砍了几截子好木头，用斧头、切刀、凿子做了个杠头。铧也是用硬木头削成的。他拔了些马莲，搓成绳子，给牛套起来耕地，真是顶上几个人挖。

Cowherd got up early next morning and thought to himself: "For farmers, where there is a piece of field, there is hope." But how could he cultivate the land without a hoe? Worried and depressed, he walked out of the shed and spotted a hoe just several steps away. He picked it up and set himself to work immediately. He dug and dug

---

① 杠头：犁。

tirelessly till dusk thickened to darkness before he stopped to rest. The third morning when he got up, he again thought to himself: "The land is flat and the soil is soft. I can plough the field." so he hacked down several more trees and made a plough with the wood, then matched it with a ploughshare made of sharpened hard wood. With some stalks of iris ensata pulled from the field, Cowherd twisted solid cord and looped it around the ox's neck. Sure enough, ploughing was much quicker then by manpower.

这么着，牛郎两天就开了一大片荒地。他先把带来的麦子种上。后来又用那斧头、切刀、凿子做了木锨、连枷啥的。算是庄稼务上了，家事也大体齐整了。他看着庄稼长着，抽时间又在崖跟前打了一眼窑，住进去，把草棚移在窑跟前，给牛卧。又砍了些柳条编了个窑门的门扇，编了个牛棚的门扇；砍了些竹子，编成箩筐、簸箕、篅^①。他一天也不闲，家事越来越齐整。

In this way, Cowherd cultivated large tracts of field and planted wheat on it. One by one, he made wooden spade, wooden flail and other farming tools. Now that he had hastily settled down with wheat planted and the daily needs met, Cowherd started to dig out a cave-house for himself on the mountainside. When it was done, he moved in, and moved the shed to the cave entrance to serve as a cow pen. He first knitted a door with willow twigs for his cave-house and another one for the cow pen, then made some cases, wicker baskets and giant grain holders with bamboo. He was busy and occupied all day long in making a cozy and comfortable home for himself.

---

① 篅：又作圌，用竹子编成的圆囤，用于存放粮食。

夏收后的一天，他提了些新麦去看哥嫂。他想是他哥哥的那些面让他一春没有饿肚子，是他哥给的粮食，才让他有了这么好的收成。他也惦记着关心他的麻姐姐，不知道她咋样了。

After the summer harvest, he went to visit his brother and sister-in-law with newly harvested grain. He was grateful to his brother for the grain his brother gave him at his departure. The grain helped him out of spring shortage of food and brought him the good harvest now. He missed his dear Sister Ramie who had always been so nice to him too.

他哥看见他，高兴得啥一样的，说常想去寻他，只是不知道到哪里去了，没地方寻。他哥最后说："兄弟，你该娶妇人了。你有了妇人，我就全放下这片心了，死了的爹、娘也就安心了。"

His brother was overwhelmed with joy at the sight of him and said he had always been thinking of looking for him, but had no clues on his whereabouts. His brother concluded the conversation at last with: "My dear brother, it's high time you got yourself a wife. Once this was done, I will worry no more about you and our parents in heaven will rest in peace."

他嫂子一看牛郎这么能干，也跑出来说了几句夸赞的话。他去看麻姐姐，麻姐姐又高兴又亲热，也劝他快一点娶个妇人，还说："你娶新媳妇儿要叫我呢，我帮你办喜事！"

Seeing that Cowherd fared quite well, his sister-in-law put on a different face and piled praise on him. When Cowherd went to Sister

Ramie's place, he was greeted with an especially warm welcome. Sister Ramie urged him to get married soon as well, saying: "You must let me know before you are going to get married. I will take care of the wedding affairs for you!"

牛郎回来，天也黑了。牛郎把看他哥嫂、麻姐姐时大家说的话也都给黄牛说了，最后说："我不想要妇人，我只想和你一起过！"那老牛摇着头说："哞——！哞——！"不过金铃能听来牛是在说"不——！不——！"他就对牛说："那像我这样只会种庄稼的人，谁跟啊？"那牛两眼看着他说："有——！有——！"牛郎高兴地说："那我就靠你了！"那牛也好像很高兴地摆着头说："好——！好——！"

When Cowherd got back home after the day's visit, it was already dark. He told the old ox everything his brother and Sister Ramie had said and concluded: "I need nobody but you!" But the now old ox shook its head in disagreement and mooed several times which Cowherd understood as "No! No!". He then said to the old ox sullenly: "Even if I do need a wife, is there any girl who would like to marry a farmer like me?" The ox gazed at him and mooed again as if saying "Yes". Cowherd patted its head cheerily: "All right, I will count on you for that!" And the old ox mooed again, "Sure! Sure!"

有一天，牛郎早早起来想去砍柴，先去开牛圈，听见那老牛在牛棚里说："早点回来，有喜事。"牛郎说："我能有啥喜事？"老牛说："领你去看好媳妇，领一个妇人回来。"牛郎说："哪里有好媳妇儿等我领？是不是老天爷可怜我，从天上掉下来一个？"老牛说："正是天上下来的。今儿有一群仙女在河里洗澡，衣裳都放在河边的石头上，你看到当中有一套红衣裳就藏起来，好事就成了。"牛郎牢牢记在心里。

One morning, when Cowherd opened the ox stall and was about to leave home to cut firewood, the ox said: "Today is your lucky day. Come back home early." Cowherd asked curiously: "My lucky day? What good luck can it be?" The old ox answered: "I will take you to your wife." At that Cowherd was even more curious: "Are you kidding me? Where is my wife? If there is one, it must be a fairy lady dropped from the sky by the Jade Emperor out of his pity on me." "Exactly!" The ox nodded: "A group of fairies are going to take a bath in the river today. They will leave their dresses on a riverside rock. Pick out the red one and put it away, then you will have a wife." Keeping every word in mind, Cowherd left home to cut firewood.

牛郎就在近处砍了一点柴，早早回来，就跟着黄牛走。那牛走到一条大河跟前停下来不走了，朝着上游远处看，只见前面水边石头上有一些红的、黄的、紫的、绿的各色鲜艳的衣裳，那水里头一些姑娘在洗澡。牛郎想起老牛的话，在树林里悄悄走过去，把石头上的一件红衣裳扯下来，藏在一个大石头背后。

He didn't go far. Once done with his work, he went back home and followed the old ox out of his house and onto road again. They went and went till they stopped by a wide river. The old ox looked up the river. Surely, by the river, there was a pile of colorful dresses of green, red, yellow and purple on a piece of rock! Several young ladies were bathing and playing in it. Keeping what the ox had said in his mind, Cowherd sneaked through the woods, pulled the red dress out of the pile, tugged it into his globe and hid himself behind a big rock.

　　过了一阵子，牛郎听见一个仙女说："洗好了也该回去了，太迟了王母知道了可了不得！"接着听见吵吵闹闹找衣裳、穿衣裳的声音。过了一阵听见一个说："我先上了。"又一个说："我也先上了。"接二连三地，牛郎抬头看见一朵一朵云彩上面都站着一个仙女升到天上去了。忽然，牛郎听见一个仙女说："我的衣裳咋寻不着了？"一个说："细心点寻，看风刮到啥地方了。"又说："快一点，太阳一偏西，王母就要派仙官查看来了，我也先走了。"

　　A while later, a young girl's voice sounded: "We are done with bathing. Let's go back now. You don't want to get into trouble, do you?" There was then a big fuss of looking for their dresses and putting them on. Then a girl said: "I'm ready to be off now." Another one followed: "I'm ready too. Let's go together." And off they went. One by one, the fairies left by riding on cloud and ascended into the sky. Then a girl's voice full of anxiety sounded: "Where's my dress? It's nowhere to be seen." Another girl comforted her: "Don't worry and look carefully. It must have been blown off the rock by the wind." She then urged: "Be quick! The heavenly official will patrol here on the order of the Queen Mother of the West before sunset. I have to go now!" With that the girl left, too.

　　看来只有那丢了衣裳的仙女一个了，牛郎便走出来说："仙女，你莫怕，你的衣裳在这搭哩！"那仙女扯着一条手巾堵在身前，说："快还给我！快还给我！"牛郎说："我听老人说，女娃子的身子不能叫人看着，谁看着了就要嫁给人家呢。今儿我看着了，你还不嫁我？别的仙女都早就上天了，你后面去，说不定还要受罚呢！"

七夕文化透视 ▸▸▸
The Cowherd and the Weaver Fairy
A Study on the Folk Story and Double Seventh Day

Now it seemed that the only girl left behind was the owner of the red dress. Cowherd came out from behind the rock, showed her the dress and said: "Fairy lady, don't be afraid. Here's your dress." The girl hastily covered herself up with a piece of towel and asked for her dress. Cowherd then said: "It's said that if a girl's body is exposed to the eyes of a man, the girl has to marry him. Now I've seen yours, how can you go without marrying me? Anyway, all your friends are back now except you. You will be punished for being late."

这时候，那老黄牛也走过来，把那仙女的衣裳用角顶上，走到仙女跟前，让仙女穿上，又抬起头看着仙女，像给仙女说啥话一样。过了一阵，那仙女就对牛郎说："那好吧，我答应你。"牛郎一听比天上掉下来一座金山还高兴。他们就一起回了家。这时候她才给牛郎说，她是玉帝和王母娘娘的外孙女，在天上织云锦，大家都叫她"织女"。

Then the old ox came over, took the dress from Cowherd's hand with its horn and gave it to the fairy lady. It looked up at her for a while as if he was communicating with her in some way. Soon enough, it seemed the fairy lady was persuaded: "All right. I will go with you." Cowherd was so pleased that he felt as if he had got a golden hill. When they got back to Cowherd's, the girl told him that she was the granddaughter of the Jade Emperor and Queen Mother of the West. Her task was to weave colorful clouds in heaven, hence was dubbed as "Weaver Fairy" up there.

牛郎、织女一到家，织女就把窑里里外外打扫得干干净净。

牛郎把家里多余的粮食拿到集市上卖掉，买来了碗、碟、灯台、针线啥的。

Weaver Fairy cleaned up the cave-house in and out once they got home. Cowherd took the extra grain to the market in exchange for needles, threads, bowls, plates, lamp stands and other household stuff.

5 桑树湾和卧牛嘴

Section 5　The Mulberry Bay and the Corner of Crouching Ox

牛郎和织女有一天经过一个山湾，看到一个桑树上爬着好些蚕。织女取来簸箕、箩筐，里头放了些桑叶，把蚕全部捡在里面，都端回家。那桑树也多，蚕长得快，当年就收了不少丝。这个地方就是现在的桑树湾。

One day, when Cowherd and Weaver Fairy passed by a bay near their home, they found many silkworms on a mulberry tree. After lining the bottom of a wicker basket with mulberry leaves carefully, Weaver Fairy collected all the silkworms from the tree and put them into the wicker basket, then went back home. There were a lot of mulberry trees around there, so the silkworms grew up quickly. Several months later, they were blessed with a good harvest of silk. It was since then the place took on the name "Mulberry Bay".

牛郎给织女说，麻姐姐是捻麻线、织麻布的能手，周围多少个村庄没有赶得上的，织女说："干脆把麻姐姐请来，住得近一点好商量，相互教。"牛郎就跑了一趟，一来给哥嫂说有了妇人，二来把麻姐姐请了来。

When Weaver Fairy heard that Sister Ramie was known far and wide for her superior craftsmanship in ramie products making, she talked it over with Cowherd: "Why don't we invite Sister Ramie over to live here? When we live next door to each other, we could help and learn from each other more conveniently." Willingly, Cowherd went back to where his brother and Sister Ramie lived to inform his brother of his wedding and to invite Sister Ramie over.

牛郎借了他哥的牛车，把纺车、织布机，锅、碗、勺啥的一下全拉来了，织女和麻姐姐一见面，亲热得象姊妹一样。他们三下两下把麻姐姐的纺车、织布机支了起来，麻姐姐做了一阵让织女看，织女也着实夸了一番。可织女纺的是丝线、织的是锦，这种纺麻、织麻布的机子用不成。

Cowherd put all Sister Ramie's stuff on an oxcart, which he had borrowed from his brother, to move to mulberry bay. Feeling like old friends at their first meeting, Sister Raime and Weaver Fairy set up the loom and the spinning wheel right away to demonstrate their weaving skills to each other. Weaver Fairy thought highly of Sister Ramie's spinning wheel and the loom, but what she was accustomed to spinning was silk thread, and what she was used to weaving was brocade, to which Sister Ramie's spinning wheel and the loom weren't very helpful.

织女请来一个木匠，请木匠照着做了一台纺丝线的纺车、

一台织锦的机子。那麻姐姐就在北面长了些白杨树的山下安了家，种上了麻。她也学织女用丝织花样的手法，在门帘、褡裢上织上花边，你看现在麻布褡裢上有蓝的、黑的、红的花纹，就是麻姐姐传下来的手艺。

Weaver Fairy then asked a carpenter to make her a machine for silk thread spinning and another one for brocade weaving. Sister Ramie settled down at the foot of the hill to the north, where there were many white poplars. Later, she planted ramie plants around where she lived. Learning from Weaver Fairy, she decorated curtains and long container pouches with beautiful lace. The blue, black and red patterns found on ramie pouches today were passed down from Sister Ramie.

织女织的锦拿到集市上去，人们都围着看，那些官府的人和商户家也都抢着要。周围村庄一些女孩儿、远处一些想学织锦巧手艺的人，也都寻着来，让织女教，织女也都给细心教。有些家道差一些、备办不起丝线纺车和织锦机的，就到麻姐姐那里去学纺麻线、织麻布的手艺。来学艺的女孩儿们和远近的人，说起织女都叫"巧娘娘"，认为她简直像神一样。

Every time Weaver Fairy went to the market, people swarmed to take a look at the brocade which would be sold out in no time as the rich such as government officials and merchants competed to buy it. With her fame spread far and wide, girls and women from villages near and far inquired about her and came for instruction. Weaver Fairy willingly imparted her skills to all of them. For those who were too poor to afford a spinning wheel or a loom for silk spinning or weaving, they went to Sister Ramie for ramie spinning and weaving. Because of her outstanding craftsmanship, Weaver

七夕文化透视 ▶▶▶
The Cowherd and the Weaver Fairy
A Study on the Folk Story and Double Seventh Day

Fairy became an idol and was affectionately called "Queen Qiao" by girls, women and the people, which means "Nimble-fingered Lady" in Chinese.

因为那地方最早只有牛郎家一口窑，就把那地方叫"牛家窑"。有些中等人家里只有女儿，还有的人家虽然也有儿子，但对女儿惯得很，就为了女儿学织锦，搬到牛郎家附近，那地方人家也就多起来，盖了些瓦房。麻姐姐种了麻的那地方，现在叫杨麻村，旁边那座山叫杨麻山。

As Cowherd's family was the first to settle down and dug the first cave-house there, the place was called Cowherd's Cave. Families with daughters fond of spinning and weaving moved there on their daughters' request, gradually turning this place into a village. More and more tile-roofed houses were built. The area where Sister Ramie once planted ramie is now called "Ramie Village", and the mountain at the foot of which Sister Ramie lived is called "Ramie Mountain".

在织女和牛郎成婚后的三年内，织女先后生了两个娃，一儿一女。和牛郎一起长大的那头老牛在草滩上吃草的时候忽然病倒起不来了。牛郎从来到世上就是和这头牛一起长大的，看得比亲人还亲。他要去请兽医，老牛说："不要请了，我的阳寿到了。要活到明年，就要增加罪过呢。我死了以后，你把我的皮剥下来，放好，如有啥事发生，你把我的皮披上，可以救急。"说完牛就咽气了。

Three years after they got married, Weaver Fairy gave birth to a boy, then a daughter. The ox, which had grown up with Cowherd since its birth and had accompanied him through all the tough times,

was now very old. One day it fell ill suddenly while grazing by the mountainside. Connected to the ox like a family, Cowherd wasted no time in sending for a vet. However, the ox stopped him and said: "I have completed my time on earth. Extending it for another year against the law of nature will incur sin on me. After my death, remove my hide and put it away in case of emergency. It will come in handy." With that the ox died.

牛郎掉着眼泪给牛磕了几个头，按牛说的把牛皮剥下来，把尸体埋了。埋那老牛的地方，现在叫"卧牛嘴"。山嘴下面的那个滩叫卧牛滩。

In tears, cowherd knelt down, kowtowed several times to the old ox, peeled off its hide and buried it. The place where the ox was buried is now called "the Corner of Crouching Ox", and the stretch of land under it is called the "Benchland of Crouching Ox".

6 牛郎织女天河会

Section 6   The Reunion of Cowherd and Weaver Fairy over the Milky Way

地上一年，天上一天。牛郎织女在一起总共过了三年，也就是天上的三天。喜鹊在秋收后上天报告收成的时候[①]，一路喊："织女下凡，喜结良缘，教人纺织，胜当神仙！"被王母娘娘派去查看织锦事务的仙官听见了，报告给王母，王母把众仙女叫

----

① 初秋时西北一些地方有一段时间见不到喜鹊，民间传说喜鹊是上天报告收成去了。

七夕文化透视 ▶▶▶
The Cowherd and the Weaver Fairy
A Study on the Folk Story and Double Seventh Day

来问，众仙女知道瞒不住，只好如实说了。王母气得要命，命令一位天将领了天兵，到汉水上游去抓织女回来。

One year on earth was equivalent to a day in heaven. Therefore, the three years they lived together were actually only three days in heaven. In the autumn of the third year, magpies that had flown into heaven to report the year's harvest warbled along their way flying upward: "Descending down to the ground, her right man Weaver Fairy finally found. Spinning, Weaving and Tutoring, her life is more than satisfactory!" Alarmed, the fairy official on patrol hurriedly reported this to the Queen Mother, who immediately summoned the fairy ladies to her palace. Knowing that Weaver Fairy's secret could no longer be kept, the fairy ladies confessed the whole thing. Queen Mother got so furious that she sent a celestial general with an army to bring Weaver Fairy back.

那天兵天将驾云到了牛家窑上空，看到牛郎正帮织女缠丝线。那天将叫天兵打了几下天鼓，晃了几下风火镜，雷震天响，闪电像一把大刀子如飞地在天上扫过。牛郎赶快把线盘给了织女，到场上去收拾晒着的麦捆子。

The celestial general and his army arrived above Cowherd's Cave, riding on cloud. They found Cowherd helping Weaver Fairy rolling silk threads onto a scroll. Following the general's order, the celestial soldiers sounded heavenly drums and rocked the wind and thunder mirror. The whole universe trembled with rolling booming thunder and flashed with lightning. Cowherd hastily handed the thread scroll to Weaver Fairy before he hurried to the open-air granary floor to collect the wheat bundles which had been laid out for sun-drying.

看到牛郎走开，那天兵一下落到院里，把织女架上登云而起。正在门外玩的两个娃一看下来两个怪物把他娘架起就走，都哭着喊了起来，叫着"娘！娘！"，朝他娘伸手追了几步，却没办法升起来够到他们的娘。织女大喊："我的娃！我的两个娃！我不去呀！"

The celestial soldiers took the chance and swiftly seized Weaver Fairy from both sides. Riding on clouds, they ascended into the sky. Seeing that their mother being grabbed by two monsters from the sky, her two kids who were playing at the gate ran after her crying: "Mom! Mom!" but, as they were unable to ride on clouds, their mother were soon taken out of their reach and rose higher and higher into the sky. Weaver Fairy reached out towards her kids and cried: "My children! I can't leave them! Please, let go of me!"

那牛郎才走了几步，听见喊声一回头，就看到有天兵天将把织女架着腾空而起，赶快拼命跑回来。紧急中他想起牛临死时说的话，赶快把牛皮取出来披在身上，门前有两个担菜的箩筐和扁担，把两个娃前后各放了一个，担上朝前跑了两步，就腾空升起了。

Some distance away, Cowherd heard his kids screaming and his wife crying. He looked back and saw what was happening. Immediately, he turned on his heels and dashed toward his wife when the ox' last words sounded in his mind. He rushed into the cave-house, put on the ox hide and dashed out of the cave. He put his two kids in the wicker basket on either side of the carrying pole on his shoulder. Instantly, he ascended into the sky chasing after the celestial army and his wife.

七夕文化透视 ▸▸▸
The Cowherd and the Weaver Fairy
A Study on the Folk Story and Double Seventh Day

Figure 17 The Cowherd and His Kids

by Lu Haiyan

　　牛郎死命追，追到南天门上，看到王母早等在那里。那王母看到牛郎快要追上，便取下头上的簪子来，朝前一划，一下出现了一条大河，那水浪翻腾着，把牛郎和织女隔开了。

Straining every bit of his strength, Cowherd chased after them all the way to the Southern Gate of Heaven where he found Queen Mother of the West waiting. Afraid that Cowherd would overtake the celestial soldiers and Weaver Fairy, Queen Mother took a hair pin from her hair and slashed it through the air. At once a wide torrential river occurred in front of Cowherd, separating him from his wife.

Figure 18 Trying to Catch Up with His Kidnapped Wife

by Lu Haiyan

七夕文化透视 ▶▶▶
The Cowherd and the Weaver Fairy
A Study on the Folk Story and Double Seventh Day

王母向玉帝报告后，玉帝因为织女私自下凡婚配凡人违犯了天条，命她长年织锦来悔过、消罪，再不能夫妻相聚。王母又怕她偷偷越过天河会见牛郎，便收了她腾云驾雾的本事，虽在天上，却和凡人一样。这样，牛郎带着两个儿女天天在天河边上哭泣，眼泪不得干。

Upon Queen Mother's report, the Jade Emperor flied into a rage and made an announcement that Weaver Fairy, for violating heaven's laws by marrying a mortal without permission, would weave brocade all year round to atone for her sin. She was forbidden from meeting her husband and kids from then on. In case she meets Cowherd secretly, Queen Mother of the West stripped her ability of riding clouds and turned her into a fairy devoid of magic powers just like a human being. Heart broken and helpless, Cowherd and their two kids cried bitterly for their wife and mother day after day, their tears rolling down their cheeks like threaded beads.

再说那比牛郎迟几天生下来的黄牛，本是金牛星下凡。他与牛郎感情最深，当他听说织女被强行招回，又让织女不得再与牛郎见面，就去寻太白金星，说牛郎如何勤苦老实，织女在人间给无数女子、妇人教纺织、缝纫的手艺，替老天爷行好，为老天爷养民，是有功的；嫁的是凡人，可凡人也都是老天爷的子孙，并不违反天地大德，请太白金星在玉帝前帮着说说好话。

When the ox, Cowherd's dearest friend who was actually Golden Ox Star, heard the news that Weaver Fairy had been called back to the heavenly court by force, he went to the Great White Venus for help. He managed to convince the prestigious immortal how upright and hard-working Cowherd was, and how many good deeds the couple had done in honor of the heavenly court such as tutoring mortals in spinning, weaving and sewing. Though a human being was not allowed to marry a fairy, Cowherd remained a subject of the upper world apart from the fact that marrying a fairy wasn't a serious transgression of the heavenly law anyway and was thus forgivable. He pleaded with Great White Venus to put in a good word for Cowherd and Weaver Fairy in front of the Jade Emperor.

太白金星一听，觉得很有道理，又怕自己一个去说，玉皇大帝不听，就又去寻太上老君。寻着，太白金星按金牛星说的说了一遍，太上老君说："下嫁凡人，自是违犯天条。可如让夫妻永世隔离，母子永世不见，也违背阴阳合和、天伦和顺之理。你我应该上奏玉帝才是。"

Convinced by Golden Ox Star, the heavenly celebrity agreed to appeal for mercy on behalf of the couple, but said: "In case I'm not persuasive enough by myself, I will ask Lord Laojun[1] to come with me." With that he left for Laojun. After hearing out the whole story, Laojun said: "Of course it violated the heavenly law for a fairy to marry a human being on earth. But it would run counter to the law of nature, thus go against the law of life if we tore a family apart— seperating a husband from his wife and mother from her kids. Let's appeal for them in front of the Jade Emperor."

两个就一起到了灵霄宝殿，向玉皇大帝奏了一本。玉皇大帝想了一下说："按你二位的意思该咋办？"太上老君说："牛郎反正已经跟上天来了，不如把他留在天上，让他照管天下农事；牛郎、织女已经成了夫妻，至少要叫他们每年相聚一次。"

---

[1] Taishang Laojun: Another prestigious immortal in Taosim.

七夕文化透视 ▶▶▶
The Cowherd and the Weaver Fairy
A Study on the Folk Story and Double Seventh Day

They then went to the Hall of the Miraculous Mist[1] and raised the issue in front of the Jade Emperor. The Emperor pondered for a while and asked: "What's your opinion on it?" Lord Laojun answered: "Cowherd is now up here anyway. Why don't we keep him here and charge him with the duty of farming affairs on earth? Since he and Weaver Fairy are already husband and wife, they should be allowed at least one meeting a year."

玉皇大帝说："那么啥时候叫他们相会合适？"太上老君说："夏收以后、初秋以前农事稍闲，就在七月头上让他们相会吧。既已占七，顺七而行，就在七月初七那天让他们相会。"玉皇大帝也就准了。

The Jade Emperor asked again: "But when?" To that, Laojun answered: "The beginning of lunar July would be a good time, as it is just between summer harvest and the beginning of autumn when it's not a busy farming season. Now that it is the seventh month of the year, let's make it a double seventh date. July 7th would be all right." To that the Jade Emperor agreed.

两个神仙下殿以后，才想起织女已经没有了腾云驾雾的本事，怎么能渡过天河呢？想再回去上奏，怕玉帝嫌他们没完没了纠缠，一讨厌，把前面已经准了的也收回就麻烦了。太上老君说："我已经把大事办成了，剩下的这点事，你就想办法吧。"

Only when the two venerable immortals had left the Hall of Miraculous Mist did it occur to them that Weaver Fairy had lost her power of riding clouds. Then how could she meet her husband and

---

① The Hall of the Miraculous Mist (Lingxiao Baodian): It is believed to be where the Jade Emperor rules the heavenly court.

kids across the Milky Way? Daring not to go back to the emperor and challenge his patience on such a trifle in case he would revoke what he had consented to, Laojun said to the Grand White Venus: "I've helped with the hardest part. Now you have to take care of the rest by yourself." With that he left.

太白金星没办法，去寻金牛星，金牛星想了想，把喜鹊在天上传言的话说了一下。太白金星说："有了！"便把鹊王叫来说："你们在天上说了牛郎织女成亲的事，弄得人家夫妻分离，织女也不能腾云驾雾了。现在玉帝准许他们一年相会一次，只有让你们想办法了。"

Being at a loss, Great White Venus went to talk the matter over with Golden Ox Star again. After thinking for a moment, Golden Ox Star told Great White Venus about what trouble the loose-tougued magpies had caused for the couple. Great White Venus patted his own head with an exclamation: "There you go!" He summoned the king of magpies over and gave the order: "It was your loose tongue which caused the tragedy—the wife was taken away from her husband, and the mother from her kids. It was also because of you that Weaver Fairy lost her power of riding clouds. Now that they are allowed to meet once a year, you should make up for your mistake by making a bridge for them over the Milky Way."

鹊王便把喜鹊全召集起来说："大家在七月初七都上天来，在天河上搭桥，让织女过桥去和牛郎相会。"七月初七这一天，喜鹊就全都飞上天去搭桥，织女过桥去和牛郎相会，牛郎也等不得，急急从这一头跑过去迎接，在鹊桥上抱头痛哭起来。就因为这，每年七月七地上一只喜鹊也看不到，等七月七过了，人们再见到喜鹊时，发现喜鹊头上的毛都没有了，那就是叫牛郎织女还有他们的两个娃给踩秃了。

The king of magpies then summoned all its subjects and announced: "On lunar July 7th every year, each of us should fly to the Milky Way so that we can make a bridge with our bodies for Cowherd and the Weaver Fairy during their reunion." When the day came, magpies did make a bridge above the Milky Way, on which the excited couple dashed toward each other after a year's separation. They hugged and cried as if they would cry their hearts out. That's why you see no magpie at all on lunar July 7th, no matter where you are. When you do see them afterwards, you may find them all bald, because the head feathers have been trod off by the excited couple and their kids during their yearly reunion.

Figure 19 Meeting over the Magpie Bridge

by Lu Haiyan

喜鹊往天上飞以前要在一个山湾里聚起来，那个地方现在叫"野鹊湾"。为啥现在人娶媳妇子都爱在屋里贴上喜鹊的画

儿，就因为喜鹊爱报喜，最后又为牛郎织女成就了好事。七月七下雨，那就是织女、牛郎的眼泪。

Every year, before magpies fly to the Milky Way to fulfil their duty on lunar July 7th, they convene in a valley now called "Magpie Valley". Why do people put up posters with magpies in bridal chamber as a custom? Because even from ancient times, magpies were known for their quick nature in reporting wedding news and it was magpies which finally brought the separated couple together every year. Why does it rain as a routine on lunar July 7th? They are tears rolling down from the couple's eyes.

织女和牛郎见面以后，就给麻姐姐托了梦，说他们相会了，她想念麻姐姐，想念人间的众姐妹，叫大家用心纺织针线，学伶俐一些，学会勤俭，就能找一个好婆家。因此，今天每次乞巧都要请麻姐姐，通过麻姐姐问巧娘娘有啥吩咐。

After their meeting over the magpie bridge, Weaver Fairy showed herself in Sister Ramie's dream and told her how much she missed her and all her friends on earth. She urged them to practice harder in spinning and weaving to become smarter and more nimble-fingered. She also advised girls and young women to remain thrifty and organized in running household affairs so that they could lead a happy life. That's why during the age-old Qiqiao celebrations, girls seek the presence of Sister Ramie, as she is the one who delivers them instructions and prophecies from the Nimble-fingered Lady, also known as Queen Qiao or Weaver Fairy.

麻姐姐种麻、纺麻线的地方现在叫麻子坝，那里的麻长得好。原先那里人织麻布、做门帘等麻布制品的手艺也高，后来只知道种麻子榨油了，倒把纺麻线、织麻布的手艺忘得差不多。

The area where Sister Ramie used to plant ramie and spin ramie yarns is now called "Ramie Terrace". The ramie she had planted grew well, and the people living there were skillful in ramie weaving and other ramie products making such as knitting ramie curtains. Unfortunately, over time, all these skills got lost. The only ancient skill which has been preserved and passed down to modern times is the skill of ramie oil extraction.

还有，那织女在天上织锦的地方，牛郎在天上隔着河远远看织女的地方，两处影子落在了地上，落影子的地方都慢慢地高了起来。七月七鹊桥的影子也映到地上，把两处高地连接起来。七月初七，我们看那云华山的天桥，也有云影落在上面，那正是牛郎织女在相会。还有那金牛星投胎的早胜牛只生长在泾河上游，现在那里的牛依然比别处的牛个头高，毛色也黄里透红，简直像枣红马一样。毕竟，牛郎家正是从那里迁来的嘛。

Thousands of years of separation passed as Weaver Fairy wove brocade day in and day out on one side of the Milky Way while Cowherd stood gazing at his wife night after night on the other side. The places where they were cast shadows on the ground. Then little by little, the shadows rose higher and higher until they were connected by the shadow of the magpie bridge. On lunar July 7th, if you observed the foot bridge on Yunhua mountain[1], you can see clouds drifting around providing shelter for the couple's reunion. The birthplace of Cowherd and the ox is famous for a breed of ox which is obviously larger and stronger than other breeds. With fur that is yellow tinged with red, the oxen there resemble bay horses. Anyway, this is the birthplace of Golden Ox Star.

---

① Yunhua mountain: a moutain in Xihe country.

Bilingual Table of Book Titles

B

《白氏经史事类》 *Encyclopedic Compilation of Best Bits from Classics and Historical Records by Bai Juyi*

《拜月亭》 *The Moon-Worship Pavilion*

《本草纲目》 *Compendium of Materia Medica*

《博物志》 *The Encyclopedic Records*

C

《崇正同人系谱》 *Chongzheng Genealogical Chart of Hakka*

《重修灵台县志·风俗节序》 "The Preface to Local Festivals and Customs" in *The Renewed County Annals of Lingtai*

《重修镇原县志·民族志》 "The Local Nationalities" in *The Renewed Edition of the County Annals of Zhenyuan*

《春渚纪闻》 *The Notes by Riverside in Spring*

D

《杜甫诗集》 *The Poetry of Du Fu*

《帝京景物略》 *The Ways and Folk Customs in the Capital*

《帝京岁时纪盛·七夕》 "On July 7th" in *Notes on Customs around the Year in the Capital*

七夕文化透视 ▶▶▶
The Cowherd and the Weaver Fairy
A Study on the Folk Story and Double Seventh Day

《东京梦华录》*Records of Folk Customs in Kaifeng the East Capital*

《董永和七仙女》*"Dong Yong and the Seventh Fairy Lady"*

《董永遇仙记》*"Dong Yong's Encounter with a Fairy"*

E

《尔雅·释天》"The Illustrations on Astronomical Vocabulary" in *Erya*

F

《风俗通义》*A General Introduction to Folk Customs*

《风土记》*The Records of Regional Folk Customs*

《风土岁时》*The Local Customs and Yearly Celebrations*

风、雅、颂 Ballads (feng), Court Hymns (ya), and Eulogies (song)

G

《高陵县志·礼仪抄略》"A Sketchy Introduction to Rituals and Customs" in *The County Annals of Gaoling*

《古今图书集成》*An Extensive Collection of Literature of All Times*

《古诗十九首》*The 19 Classical Poems*

《癸辛杂识续集》*A Sequel to Miscellaneous Notes from Guixin Street of Ling'an*

《广东新语·事语》"Customs and Events" in *New Notes about Guangdong*

H

《汉书·百官志》"An Introduction to Official Posts" in *The Book of the Han Dynasty*

《汉书·律历志》"The Record of Music and Calendar" in *The Book of the Han Dynasty*

《汉书·天文志》"The Record of Astronomy" in *The Book of the Han Dynasty*

《汉书·武帝纪》"A Biography of Emperor Wu" in *The Book of the Han Dynasty*

《汉武故事》*The Story about Emperor Wu of the Han Dynasty*

《淮南方华术》*The Beauty Tips of Huainan*

《淮南万毕术》*An Exhaustive Records of Mystic Techniques by Huainan Zi*

《淮南子·说山》"On the Overwhelming Vital Principle of the Way" in *Huainan Zi*

《黄帝内经》*The Yellow Emperor's Classic of Internal Medicine*

J

《荆楚岁时记》*The Festivals and Folk Customs of the Jing and Chu Area*

K

《开元天宝遗事》*A Memoir on Kaiyuan and Tianbao Years of the Tang Dynasty*

《括地志》*Kuodi Zhi*

L

《礼记·月令》"The Lunar Months" in *The Book of Rites*

《离骚》"The Departing Sorrows"

《列仙传》*The Biographies of Fairies*

《陇东风俗》*The Folk Customs of Eastern Gansu Province*

《吕氏春秋》*A History by Lü Buwei*

P

《平凉府风俗考》*A Study on Folk Customs in Prefecture Pingliang*

Q

《鹊桥仙》"Magpie-bridge Fairy"

R

《日书》*The Almanac*（*The Book of Days*）

《日下旧闻考》*The Collated Records on Peking's History and Culture*

《容斋随笔》*Writings from Rongzhai Study*

《入蜀记》*On the Years in Sichuan*

S

《三辅黄图》*Sanfu Huangtu*

《山海经》*The Classic of Mountains and Seas*

《山海经·海内经》"Inland Part" in *The Classic of Mountains and Seas*

《尚书·禹贡》"The Tribute of Yu" in *The Book of Documents*

《世本》*The Book of Pedigree*

《史记集解》*The Annotations to Records of the Grand Historian*

《史记·律书》"On Rules and Principles" in *Records of the Grand Historian*

《史记·秦本纪》"The History of the Qin Dynasty" in *Records of the Grand Historian*

《史记·天官书》"The Profiling of Officials in Heaven" in *Records of the Grand Historian*

《诗经·国风》"Ballads of the States" in *The Book of Songs*

《诗经·小雅》"Classic of Poetry" in *The Book of Songs*

《诗经原始》*Literary Research on The Book of Songs*

《说郛》*Shuofu*

《四民月令》*A Handbook and Calendar for Farming*

《搜神记》*Anecdotes about Spirits and Immortals*

《岁华纪丽》*A Record of Folk Customs in Four Seasons*

《岁时广记》*An Extensive Collection of the Yearly Festivals and Customs*

《岁时杂记》*Notes on Yearly Festival and Customs*

T

《天问》"Interrogations against the Heaven"

《太平御览》*Imperial Readings of the Taiping Era*

《唐书·百官志》"An Introduction to Official Posts" in *The Book of the Tang Dynasty*

W

《万历野获编》*A Casual Talk on Ways of the World during Wanli Years*

《韦氏月录》*Monthly Records by Madame Wei*

《武林旧事》*A Miscellaneous Records of History*

《梧桐雨》*Wutong Yu / Drizzles on Chinese Parasol*

X

《西安府祠庙考》*A Study on Temples and Ancestral Halls of Xi'an*

七夕文化透视 ▸▸▸
The Cowherd and the Weaver Fairy
A Study on the Folk Story and Double Seventh Day

Postscript by the Translator

　　牛郎织女故事在中国古代四大民间传说中，是孕育历时最久、形成时间最早、流传范围最广的传说，而与该故事紧密联系的七夕节自古以来就是民间最重要的节庆之一。牛郎织女故事孕育于汉水上游①，形成于西北。织女形象的原型应是秦人的始祖女修，而牛郎（牵牛）的形象应是周人的祖先叔均。随着时间的推移，牛郎织女故事逐渐传播开来，并产生了分化，形成各地细节各异的牛郎织女故事，进而演绎出相关的七夕节俗。

　　关于"牛郎""织女"的最早记载见于《诗经·小雅·大东》，经过两汉时期的发展，魏晋南北朝时期牛郎织女故事框架基本形成。《诗经》中的《周南·汉广》和《秦风·蒹葭》其实也反映了早期牛郎织女的传说②。汉代《古诗十九首》"迢迢牵牛星"一首、《玉台新咏》中所收汉代故事"兰若生春阳"也都是写牛郎织女传说的。③自南北朝时期起，牛郎织女故事主要在

---

① 今西汉水上游。西汉以前西汉水与东汉水为一条水，后由于地震，其上游流至今略阳以西遇堵塞而南折流入今嘉陵江，其重要支流沔水遂又名"东汉水"，其上游部分改名"西汉水"。参见赵逵夫：《〈周南·汉广〉探微》，《古典文学知识》2010 年第 3 期；赵逵夫：《〈秦风·蒹葭〉新探》，《文史知识》2010 年第 8 期。

② 参见赵逵夫：《〈周南·汉广〉探微》，《古典文学知识》2010 年第 3 期；赵逵夫：《〈秦风·蒹葭〉新探》，《文史知识》2010 年第 8 期。

③ 参见赵逵夫：《再论"牛郎织女"传说的孕育形成和早期分化》，《中华文史论丛》2009 年 4 月总第 96 期。

七夕文化透视 ▶▶▶
The Cowherd and the Weaver Fairy
A Study on the Folk Story and Double Seventh Day

两个层面传播：一是文人层面的传播，二是民间传播[①]。东汉末年、西晋东晋之间、唐末、宋末等的几次战乱中，大批北方世家大族南迁（即后代所谓客家）对牛郎织女传说的南播起了一定作用，故今天该传说在南方带有古代贵族社会的特征（如织女找到仙衣并离家，牛郎快追上她时，她拔下簪子划出一道银河将自己与牛郎隔开，这一情节与《古诗十九首》"迢迢牛郎星"中说织女"纤纤擢素手，札札弄机杼，终日不成章，泣涕零如雨"的情形并不一致）。从此，牛郎织女故事在中华大地上可谓遍地生花，拥有了情节各异的版本，有些甚至传播到了一些少数民族地区，并因此带上了当地的民族文化特色。此外，历史上中华文化强大的对外辐射力使得很多东亚、东南亚国家也有着牛郎织女故事流传的痕迹，如日本不同地区流传的"天女下凡""七夕""养犬星与七夕星"等故事、朝鲜的"牛郎织女星"故事、韩国的"仙女与樵夫"故事、越南的"织女和牛郎"故事、菲律宾的"七仙女"故事，以及印度尼西亚和马来西亚各种丰富多彩的羽衣型传说。在这些故事中，有一些还留有非常明显的中国文化元素的印迹；有一些则表现出很多本土文化元素；而另一些由于殖民历史等原因，在牛女故事框架基础上包裹了浓厚的西方文化色彩（如羽衣型传说）。从这些数目众多、姿态各异的流传故事变体中，我们不仅得以一窥文化传播的复杂过程，也能感受到这个故事本身的持久魅力。

在翻译该牛郎织女故事的过程中，我发现了它与世界文化的两点相通之处：一、与西方羽衣型/天鹅处女型故事（swan maiden）的相似性；二、与西方文学中"孤岛"或曰"荒岛求生"母题的相似性。羽衣型/天鹅处女型故事是在欧洲流传很广的一类故事，其共同"要素"（母题，motif）主要有：（1）天

[①] 参见赵逵夫：《有关小说〈牛郎织女〉及其校订的几个问题》，《〈牛郎织女〉阅定本后记》，载佚名著，赵子贤阅定，赵逵夫点校：《牛郎织女》，甘肃人民出版社 2011 年版，第 138-139 页。

鹅脱了羽衣，变成天女（人之女性）而沐浴；（2）男人盗匿羽衣，迫天女与之结婚；（3）结婚后，生产若干儿女；（4）生产儿女之后，夫妇关系破裂，天女升天；（5）破裂原因是发现了此前为了"结婚原因"被藏匿的羽衣。这类故事变体繁多，形式多样，几乎在世界各国民间传说中都能找到影子，其中尤以欧洲神话传说中的数量之多和流传之广为最。本书所译的牛女故事系列是中国西北，或者更确切说在秦人的发源地甘肃西和、礼县流传的版本，可以明显看出上述的前四个要素，尽管首尾要素"脱掉羽衣变女沐浴"和"夫妇关系破裂，天女升天"与本书牛女故事中的情节有出入。据我查阅的英文资料来看，西方有关羽衣型/天鹅处女型故事的叙述和研究鲜少提及中国的此类故事，不知是由于故事起源和内涵差异导致的隔阂，还是纯粹出于文化传播的阻碍。关于世界范围内该故事的起源，有两个问题值得我们思考：一、世界各地的此类传说是分别形成的还是从单一起源传播开的？二、不论是单一起源经由文化传播扩散开来，还是世界各地同时形成这样的一个故事，它形成的原因是什么？是什么原因导致它在各异的文化中生生不息，历久弥新？就像世界民间文学中广泛存在的"灰姑娘"主题（中国"叶限"故事①）一样，这是一个有趣的现象。同样，在本书牛女故事系列的第4个故事"牛郎织女成夫妻"中，有牛郎分家之后离家开荒、自给自足的故事情节，并且对此过程的描写非常详细。这与西方文学中屡见不鲜的"孤岛/荒岛求生"故事有很高的相似性，只不过在中国的故事版本中表现为被亲情背叛、孤苦无依的主人公在荒芜环境中艰难求生，最终独立自主的故事。西方海洋型生活环境中的孤岛只是一种生存环境的象征，它代表着人类的孤独和人生的艰难挑战着个人的能力和信念。这类故事告诉我们，即使在被社会抛弃、孤立无援的情

---

① 参见唐代段成式《酉阳杂俎》续集《支诺皋》中的"叶限"故事，情节与格林童话中的"灰姑娘/辛德瑞拉"故事相似度极高。

况下，人也应该努力地把孤岛改造成乐园，踏踏实实地居家过日子，用自己的努力换来衣食无忧以及后面的好运。从这一点来看，该系列牛郎织女故事和欧洲充满现实主义冒险精神和个人英雄主义的"鲁滨逊漂流记"类型的故事，有着深层的精神联结，在世界文化中跨越时空表达着相同的人文精神。我想，这是牛郎织女故事尤为可贵的一点。

基于对牛郎织女故事的喜爱和多姿多彩、历史悠久的七夕节俗的兴趣，我动手编译了这本书。翻译过程中难度最大的是乞巧歌的翻译，一是歌曲中含有大量西北特色的方言词汇，二是诗歌的翻译实在不是我所擅长：既要言简意丰地表达民歌中的意蕴，还要在音韵上还原歌谣之美，实在是太大的挑战。几经修改，译出的成果哪怕仍不尽如人意，但也已倾我所能，希望大家批评指正。

我对于牛郎织女故事的兴趣始于我祖父和父亲的相关研究，目前成书的主要部分选自我父亲赵逵夫的著作《七夕文化透视》。为了突出民俗文化内容和保证可读性，本书主要选取了原书中牛郎织女故事的起源和七夕节俗内容的部分加以翻译，文献研究及考古发现等学术性过强的部分省略未译。后附的牛郎织女故事选自我父亲另外两部著作《西和乞巧节》和《中国女儿节·西和乞巧文化》等的有关章节。

由于我博士阶段从事跨文化传播的研究，且长期在高校从事翻译教学和翻译实践，因此作为一种文化传播的实践，我很愿意将中国的牛郎织女故事和七夕节俗介绍给外国读者，使更多人感受我们民族文化的魅力，从而更好地了解"民族的就是世界的"这一命题。

Among the four most famous Chinese folk stories, "The Cowherd and the Weaver Fairy" boasts the longest history and has been known and told by the largest population since ancient

times. The festival closely related to the folk story is one of the most important festival in China. The story originated in the upper reaches of the Han River in northwestern China, where two of the earliest Chinese tribes Qin and Zhou inhabited. The Weaver Fairy is actually the remotest female ancestor, Nüxiu, of the Qin Tribe and the Cowherd is the male ancestor of the Zhou Tribe. As the living areas of the two tribes expanded and communication increased, legends about their respective ancestors started to merge, providing the ground for the formation of a new story that would later be known as "The Cowherd and the Weaver Fairy". As the story spread, it was localized and started to take on new details which varied from place to place. When its influence grew, people started to celebrate it as a festival, with specific customs developed.

The earliest record of "the Cowherd" and "the Weaver Fairy" can be found in "Dadong" in *The Book of Songs*, which was written during the Spring and Autumn period. Further developed during the Western and Eastern Han Dynasties, the story finally came into being around the Northern and Southern Dynasties, though many poems had already suggested the existence of the plot or characters before that. Since then, the folk story has been passed down in two social classes: one among upper-class intellectuals and the other among lower-class ordinary working people at large.

Hakka's (the powerful, rich and well-educated people who migrated from the north to the south in ancient China) several large-scale southward migrations hastened its spread in the south, and gave it features obviously typical of the noble class, which differed in some striking details from that spread in the north.

As the story was told among an increasingly larger population and in wider areas, more and more varieties were developed, and

七夕文化透视 ▸▸▸
The Cowherd and the Weaver Fairy
A Study on the Folk Story and Double Seventh Day

details added, which in some cases differ strikingly from each other. Considering the strong influence Chinese culture had in history on other Eastern and Southeastern Asian countries, it's no wonder that similar stories exist in countries like Japan, Korea, Vietnam, the Philippines, Indonesia and Malaysia. Among these foreign varieties, some still keep distinctive features of the Chinese origin, while some others have been localized with the addition of local cultural elements. Still some others, under the influence of long-term colonial rule in history, are obviously tinted by colonial culture. From all these varieties in circulation, we can not only get a glimpse of the complicated process of cultural communication, but also feel the enduring charm of the story itself.

When translating the version of the story attached to the end of the book which is mainly told in northwestern China, that is, the birthplace of the story itself, I noticed two commonalities it shares with the world culture: Frist, its similarity to the Swan Maiden story popular all over the world, especially in European culture. Second, its resemblance to the motif manifested in the story genre titled "survival on a deserted island" in western culture. The key elements are quite similar. As far as I know, the Chinese version of the Swan Maiden story just like "The Cowherd and the Weaver Fairy" is rarely mentioned in the relevant research by Western scholars. Whether this is caused by differences in the origin and cultural connotation of the story or simply the result of insufficient communication remains a mystery.

As for its circulation, two questions deserve our attention: First, did all those varieties develop and spread from the same origin, or, were they conceived in parallel, with no actual connection at all? Second, in either case, what's the reason for its formation? What gives

it the long-lasting charm? Why did it outlive many other folk stories in diverse cultures all over the world? These questions are quite interesting and thought-provoking, just like the Cinderella stories (in China featured in a story titled "Ye Xian" [叶限] in *Youyang Zazu* by Duan Chengshi in the Tang Dynasty) loved by people all over the world, regardless of cultural background.

In "The Cowherd and the Weaver Fairy", when thrown out of his brother's house, Cowherd starts from scratch in a remote and deserted part of the land. He has no one else to rely on except himself. Yet his diligence, perseverance, and optimism eventually bring him a good harvest and a self-sufficient life. Its similarity to the "survival on a deserted island" stories, one of the most popular story genre in Western literature, lies in the belief in one's own efforts: no matter how difficult the situation is, a man can turn it around and achieve a happy ending through hard work. From this perspective we can see the hidden spiritual connection between the Chinese folk story and Robinson Crusoe stories, which highlights realistic and adventurous spirit as well as individualistic heroism. This is where the value of the Chinese folk story lies.

Out of love for the story and the interest in the colorful Qiqiao festive celebrations in my hometown, I translated part of the book of the same title by my father. Attached to it is the story told in my hometown, which was also collected and compiled by my father. Both my father and grandfather devoted themselves to the research on the folk story and the age-old Qiqiao customs that are still passionately celebrated in my hometown. My hometown was conferred the title of "The Cradle of Qiqiao Culture" in 2006 and was granted a project to preserve national intangible cultural heritage—Qiqiao culture in 2008. The translation of all the Qiqiao songs gave me a particularly

七夕文化透视 ▶▶▶
The Cowherd and the Weaver Fairy
A Study on the Folk Story and Double Seventh Day

hard time as there is a big dialect vocabulary, and I am not good at maintaining the rhyme. But I have tried my best.

I am a lecturer with School of Translation Studies at Jinan Univesity, giving lectures in Translation, Western Culture and Linguistic and Cultural Comparison between Chinese and English. I specialized in Cultural Communication during my PhD programme. I hope that my work can promote the knowledge dissemination and preservation of folk customs, thus contributing to the spread of colorful Chinese culture all over the world.

本书插图剪纸作者简介

· 卢海燕，"中国乞巧之乡"甘肃省陇南市西和县人，医务工作者，剪纸艺术大师，优秀民间艺术家。

Lu Haiyan, a medical worker born in Xihe county (the birthplace of Qiqiao Customs), a master of paper-cutting and decorative folk arts.

· 赵金慧，"中国乞巧之乡"甘肃省陇南市西和县人，退休教师，剪纸艺术传承人，优秀民间艺术家。

Zhao Jinhui, a retired teacher in Xihe county and an outstanding inheritor of local paper-cutting skills.